Beethoven's Missa Solemnis

MISSA

composita, et

SERENISSIMO AC EMINENTISSIMO

DOMINO DOMINO

RUDOLPHO JOANNI

Caesareo Principi et Archiduci Austriae S.R.E. Tit. s. Petri in monte
aureo Cardinali et Archiepiscopo Otomucenfi

profundissima cum veneratione

dedicata a

LUDOVICO van BEETHOVEN.

OPUS 123.

Ex sumtibus vulgantium.

MOGUNTIAE

ex taberna musices B. SCHOTT filiorum.

PARIS

chez les fils de B. Schott, rue De Bourbon n.° 17.

ANVERS chez A. SCHOTT.

1827.

Title-page of first edition of Beethoven's Missa Solemnis

Beethoven's Missa Solemnis

Roger Fiske

Charles Scribner's Sons
NEW YORK

Contents

MT
115
B4
F6
1979

1 The Mass in Beethoven's Day   1

2 The Missa Solemnis Composed and Performed   15

3 Beethoven as a Christian   28

4 Kyrie   32

5 Gloria   37

6 Credo   53

7 Sanctus and Benedictus   72

8 Agnus Dei   81

9 The Orchestration of the Missa Solemnis   94

10 Since Beethoven's Death   102

Notes   113

Bibliography   116

Discography   118

Index   121

Von Herzen—Möge es wieder—zu Herzen gehen!
(From the heart it comes—to the heart may it go!)

written by Beethoven
on the score

1
The Mass in Beethoven's Day

> . . . some to church repair
> Not for the doctrine but the music there

wrote Alexander Pope in 1709, and Popes in another land have regularly warned their flock against this attitude. Fine distinctions are involved. Is the purpose of church music, paintings and architecture to arouse devotion and glorify God or to distract the congregation, to make the services less boring? It is usually very difficult to decide if a piece of music is religious or not, at least as difficult as it is for a communist to decide if it is bourgeois or not, and in both cases the distinction is important because on it hangs the fate of the music. Until the 1960s and the Second Vatican Council, two considerations had regularly exercised Rome down the ages. Instruments in church other than the organ are dangerous and need strict control, and any resemblance to Italian opera must be avoided at all costs.

The first danger was of very ancient standing. As long ago as the twelfth century an Abbot of Rievaulx named Ailred wrote: 'Let me speak now of those who, under a show of religion, doe obpalliate the business of pleasure. . . Whence hath the Church so many Organs and Musicall Instruments?' While dreadful singing goes on, 'the common people standing by, trembling and astonished, admire the sound of the Organs, the noyse of the Cymballs and Musicall Instruments, the harmony of the Pipes and Cornets.'[1] The safest way of avoiding the second danger, the operatic style, was to limit church music to what was written before opera was ever invented (around 1600); that is, to plainsong and music more or less under plainsong influence. In the seventeenth and early eighteenth centuries composers in Italy often imitated the Palestrina style when setting those portions of the Mass that were traditionally sung, and the Church found such music acceptable. But the Vatican had very little control over what went on in the Austrian Empire. By the second half of the eighteenth century many Austrian composers were writing settings of the Mass with orchestral accompaniment, notably Mozart in youth and the Haydn brothers, Joseph and Michael, and they made no attempt whatever to imitate the Palestrina style. Worse still, they often seemed to be writing in the style of Italian opera.

Sometimes these composers wrote grandly for special occasions, but often their settings were intended for run-of-the-mill services which, thought the Archbishop of Salzburg, should not exceed 45 minutes in length. This limited the settings Mozart and Michael Haydn wrote for him to about 20 minutes, which meant that there could be virtually no repetition of words in the Gloria or Credo. Sometimes they saved time by having verbal phrases overlapping, and in his *Organ Solo* Mass, K.259 Mozart actually achieved a Gloria that plays for 1 minute 40 seconds; the entire Mass lasts only 13 minutes. Presumably the archbishop was in even more of a hurry that day than usual. But such settings were not always comprehensible, and years later in the Moto Proprio of 1903 Pope Pius X tried to clarify and amplify what his predecessors had ruled on the subject. As well as banning (yet again) 'the theatrical style which was in the greatest vogue, especially in Italy', he stressed that the words of the Mass should be sung 'without alteration or inversion, without repetition, without breaking the syllables'. The Gloria and Credo must not be 'composed in separate pieces. . . capable of being detached from the rest; instruments other than the organ can be allowed only with the special license of the Ordinary', and 'frivolous instruments such as drums, cymbals, bells and the like are forbidden'.

Other fears expressed in the Moto Proprio had also exercised the Catholic Church for a very long time. Around 1550 the Council of Trent had pleaded for homophonic music rather than contrapuntal so that the words of the Mass might be more clearly heard, and though Palestrina and his contemporaries seldom took much notice of this they did on occasions. It is of course understandable that the Church should want the words to be heard and in 1749 Pope Benedict XIV complained that they were being drowned by instrumental accompaniments. He thought, rather oddly, that only strings and bassoons should be allowed; other wind, and all percussion and plucked instruments, should be forbidden. But in Austria the church authorities closed their minds to these well-meant instructions. Indeed the Emperor Joseph II so resented Papal attempts to control what went on in Austria that he seriously considered breaking with Rome as Henry VIII had done. However, an enlightened liberal, he also resented some of the pronouncements of his own church authorities, and in 1783 he inadvertently pleased Rome by severely restricting the use of orchestras in Austrian churches.[2] These restrictions were lifted by his successor, but for some years they led to a great reduction in 'orchestral' Masses.

Growing up in Bonn, Beethoven must have been aware of these clashes of view if only vaguely (he was thirteen in 1783), and we need look no further for the reason that his early output includes no church music. Even when in the 1790s 'orchestral' Masses became acceptable once more, they were written in smaller quantities partly owing to financial problems caused by the Napoleonic Wars. From now on such Masses tended to be composed only for special occasions, and for us as for Beethoven the most interesting of these special occasions occurred annually in the Bergkirche at Eisenstadt some 25 miles SSE of Vienna. Though small, the church had a large enough organ loft to accommodate singers and instrumentalists, and it was the preserve of the great Esterhazy family for which Joseph Haydn had worked all his life. In the early nineties when Beethoven was his pupil Haydn had brought him to Eisenstadt but by this time his highly musical employer, Prince Nicholas Esterhazy, was dead, and his unmusical successor, Prince Anton, had greatly reduced the musical establishment. For Haydn there were compensations: he was readily given permission to make his two long visits to London. When in 1795 he returned from the second of these Prince Anton had died and been succeeded by his son, Prince Nicholas II.

The new Prince was passionately interested in the theatre, in his collection of pictures and in his mistresses, but not in music. He never got on well with Haydn or any other of the composers he employed, and it was as well that he required little else of his Kapellmeister than a new Mass every September to celebrate the Name Day of his wife. This was performed in the Bergkirche on 8 September if that were a Sunday; otherwise on the first

Sunday thereafter or at least on some day before the end of the month. Haydn wrote six of these Name Day Masses, and as he had written six others quite early in his career the late ones are now numbered 7 to 12. No.12, the most lavishly scored, was the last composition Haydn completed. He was seventy when he wrote it, and old age was lying heavily on him. The Prince, who had other composers at his beck and call, waited a year or two to see if Haydn was going to regain his strength and then, in 1804, appointed Hummel as his Kapellmeister. Years later Hummel wrote that the appointment was on Haydn's advice.

Johann Nepomuk Hummel (1778–1837) came from Bratislava on the borders of Moravia. By the turn of the century he was admired all over Western Europe as a pianist and as a composer for the piano, but when he became the Prince's Kapellmeister in 1804 he is not known to have ever written any church music. He was unable to get his first Mass finished by September but on the last day of that month he conducted in the Bergkirche a performance of Haydn's oratorio, *The Creation*, an experience that must have taught him a great deal about composing for voices. A week or two later he wrote to Haydn, who was now living a retired life in Vienna, and, addressing him as 'Most beloved Papa' and signing himself 'Your devoted Son', he enclosed a copy of his Op.13 Piano Sonata which had just been published; it was dedicated to Haydn. Hummel's affection was matched by his tact. He composed the next two Name Day Masses, but in 1807 the new Mass was commissioned from Beethoven. This is curious in that those Hummel had written are unexpectedly good, but it may well be that tensions were already building up between him and his employer. He was dismissed in 1808, recalled and dismissed again in 1811, apparently as a result of a note he had written denying that the Prince had any artistic taste.[3] It may well be that by then he wanted to be dismissed. He hated wearing his Kapellmeister's uniform, was not on very good terms with the orchestra, and must have longed to return to what he did best, public piano playing.

The Masses that Haydn and Hummel wrote for the Princess's Name Day were the models for Beethoven's Mass in C, and to a lesser degree they also influenced his Missa Solemnis. A list[4] may be helpful.

performed			*published*
1796? Haydn	No.8	*Missa St Bernardi von Offida (Heiligmesse)*, in B flat	May 1802
1797	No.7	*Missa in tempore belli (Paukenmesse)*, C	Oct 1802
1798	No.9	*Missa in angustiis (Nelson)*, D minor	May 1803
1799	No.10	*Theresienmesse*, B flat	1840
1801	No.11	*Schöpfungmesse (Creation)*, B flat	June 1804
1802	No.12	*Harmoniemesse*, B flat	Sept 1808
1806?		Mass in B flat, Op.77	c.1818
1805? Hummel		Mass in E flat, Op.80	c.1826
1807 Beethoven		Mass in C, Op.86	1812

Haydn did not write a new Mass in 1800; that September No.9 was revived in the presence of Nelson and Emma Hamilton. The *Schöpfungmesse* was so-called because Haydn quotes in it a theme from near the end of his oratorio, *The Creation*. Of the first seven Masses in the above list as many as five are in the key of B flat, the other two being in C and D, the next keys up the scale. These were then the keys most favoured by trumpeters, and in Haydn 7–10 and Hummel's B flat, trumpets were the only brass instruments and for that reason needed more consideration than usual. We shall see later that in the Missa Solemnis (which is in D) Beethoven frequently turned to the key of B flat, and at least in the Dona he did so for the sake of his trumpets and drums. The absence of horns in Haydn 7–10 is unexpected as is the absence of woodwind in 9; only clarinets are to be found in 10. The Prince had dismissed most of his wind players to save expense. Haydn sometimes added wind parts when these Masses were repeated in Vienna. His last two Masses were written during a brief interlude of peace in Europe, and it was perhaps for this reason that the Prince agreed that a full band should be engaged, but the Peace of Amiens did not hold and so Hummel was denied not only flutes, clarinets and horns in his B flat Mass but solo singers as well.

When Beethoven set about writing his Mass for the Prince he must have needed models because he had had no experience of church music since he was a boy. Four of Haydn's late Masses were by then in print and he studied some or all of these. He could also have looked at a published full score of Mozart's *Coronation* Mass, K.317 though he might have found it somewhat old-fashioned. Later when he began working on the Missa Solemnis he could also have studied Haydn's last Mass and two by Cherubini, a composer he is known to have admired. Cherubini's First Mass had been published in 1810, the second (in vocal score only) a year or so later. No.2 in D minor is remarkable for its stupefying length; it is much longer than the Missa Solemnis. Its quality is sadly variable, with banalities on the very first page, but Beethoven may well have found things to admire in it. He may also have had access to manuscript scores of Masses by his one-time teacher, Albrechtsberger; one of these had been performed at Eisenstadt shortly before Beethoven's Mass in C.

We know all too little about what music Beethoven knew and what music he liked. From about 1810 his knowledge of other composers must have been obtained entirely through his eyes. Deaf men do not go to concerts. Evidence as to what music he owned is contradictory, and there is no reason to believe all that was written on the subject by Anton Schindler (1795–1864). He and Beethoven first met in 1814, and subsequently Schindler became Beethoven's part-time secretary and eventually his Boswell. The biography he wrote (and then rewrote) is much the most interesting of the early Lives, even though it is subject to errors, concealments and even falsehoods. Schindler described Beethoven's music library as

very meagre. It contained only a very few of his own works. Of the works of the old Italian masters all he knew—all any of his contemporaries knew—was a small collection of short pieces by Palestrina, Nanini, Victoria and others that Baron von Tuscher had had published by Artaria in 1824. Beethoven owned this collection. He had nothing by Haydn or Cherubini...[5]

Schindler was either putting too much trust in an uncertain memory or relying on guesswork when he concocted the passage quoted above. Quite different information is given by Thayer in an Appendix called 'Beethoven's Estate'[6]. This shows that when he died Beethoven owned a large number of his own works in both print and manuscript; also full scores of Handel's *Messiah* and *Alexander's Feast* with Mozart's accompaniments, together with various Handel choruses he had copied out himself by way of preparation for his late choral works;* also Bach's *Art of Fugue*, four Mozart operas and the Requiem, two operas by Cherubini but no church music, Haydn's *The Creation*, *The Seasons*, and Masses 'No.1' and 'No.3' (Nos.8 and 9 according to modern numbering). All these were published full scores. In addition he was able to consult the library of his patron and friend, the young Archduke Rudolph. On 29 July 1819 Beethoven wrote to him and mentioned that he had just borrowed some useful items, and as the rest of the letter shows his mind running on Bach and Handel his borrowings surely included music by these composers, some of it no doubt in manuscript. As he was just starting work on the Missa Solemnis the reason for these borrowings is obvious. It is unlikely that he ever saw the music of Bach's B minor Mass. On 9 September 1824 he wrote for a copy to the Zurich publisher, Nageli, but it was not published until 1833, six years after Beethoven's death.

When the C major Mass was commissioned late in 1806 Beethoven must have been told in some detail what was expected of him, but no correspondence on the subject survives and perhaps there never was any. Perhaps some emissary from Eisenstadt (it could have been Hummel) knocked on the door of his lodgings and gave him the details verbally: about 45 minutes long, solo voices mingling with chorus, normal orchestra. Because of his lack of experience in this field Beethoven must surely have asked for and been lent published and manuscript full scores of Masses by Haydn, Hummel and perhaps other composers. He got his commission finished in time but only just, and he spent three days at Eisenstadt preparing for the performance. The occasion was not a success. The Prince very much disliked Beethoven's music and said so; Beethoven left in a fury. When the music was published he neither dedicated it to the Prince nor sent him a copy. In a letter to one of his mistresses the Prince described the music as 'insupportablement ridicule et détestable'. Beethoven was not invited to Eisenstadt again. Back in Vienna he started work on the Fifth and Sixth Symphonies, Op.67 and 68. The opus number of the Mass in C, 86, is deceptive and the reason merits explanation.

*The much-appreciated forty volumes of Handel's Complete Works edited by Samuel Arnold did not arrive until the Missa Solemnis was finished.

Full scores of major works can never have brought publishers a quick profit. If the major work was a Mass with orchestral accompaniment then publishers could not even hope to recoup their expenses because performances would be limited to a comparatively small area of Central Europe and even there they would be very few in number. Thus it was that composers such as Haydn were not paid when their Masses were published. Prestige alone was thought sufficient reward. The opus numbers of Hummel's Masses and of Beethoven's Mass in C are deceptively high because it took these composers a matter of years to get anyone to publish the music. This was either because they *did* expect payment or because publishers sometimes thought prestige cost them too much. In July 1808, nearly two years after the Eisenstadt performance, Beethoven wrote about his Mass in C to Breitkopf & Härtel: 'Notwithstanding the utterly frigid attitude of our age to works of this kind, the Mass is very dear to my heart.' He had received a discouraging reply to a most hard-bargaining letter to these publishers saying that they could have the Fifth and Sixth Symphonies and the A major Cello Sonata only if they would take the Mass as well: 'You say there is no demand for church works. . . but if only you will arrange a performance in Leipzig you'll find music lovers will immediately come forward and want the music. Publish it by all means in a vocal score with German words. However you do it, I guarantee its success.' But Breitkopf & Härtel did not accept the Mass until Beethoven threw in the Op.70 Piano Trios as well, and even then they did not hurry themselves. The full score did not appear until 1812.

As a concert work any Mass is a bit of an embarrassment. The only proper place for a musical setting of the Eucharist is a church, yet an elaborate special-occasion Mass with full orchestral accompaniment is quite unsuited to a church apart from the particular service for which it was written. I have traced only three performances of the Mass in C during Beethoven's lifetime and performances are still a rarity today. His *Pastoral* Symphony must be played a hundred times for every once that the Mass in C is heard, yet for me the latter is by far the greater work, the opening Kyrie and the final Agnus Dei among the great achievements of Beethoven's Middle Period. Suffering from the same initial disadvantage, the Missa Solemnis has overcome it more successfully but full justice has still not been done to either work. Beethoven's willingness to have the Mass in C published, and (as we shall see later) the Missa Solemnis performed with German words unrelated to the Eucharist, may seem shocking to us, but his great fear was that the music would never be heard at all.

Most of the conventions Beethoven adopted in his Mass in C he adopted again in the Missa Solemnis and we shall now consider just what he inherited from the past and more particularly from previous Eisenstadt Masses. We need not concern ourselves with elaborate Cantata Masses such as Bach's B minor, Haydn's *St Cecilia* Mass and Mozart's never-finished Mass in C minor. They must have been even less to Papal taste than the Masses Beethoven wrote for they all included arias and duets that could be performed on their own out of context, and the lovely 'Incarnatus est' in Mozart's Mass is flagrantly operatic in style. In his late Masses Haydn never wrote arias that could be hived off, nor did Hummel, Cherubini or Beethoven. They all set the words in the approved five (or six) movements, each of them more or less continuous. Beethoven has sometimes been credited with being the first composer to mix soloists and chorus in the same passage, but in fact Haydn does this in all his late Masses as also in *The Creation*, and so does Hummel in his Mass in E flat. In what follows, Haydn's Masses are identified by their numbers (see p.5).

Kyrie

Kyrie eleison—Christe eleison—Kyrie eleison
(Lord have mercy upon us, etc.)*

The Greek words obviously invite ternary form and in some Palestrina Masses there is a Da Capo (From the Beginning) after the middle section, but by the Viennese period a rough approximation to ternary form was usual as in Hummel's B flat and the two Beethoven Masses. Haydn showed little interest in this plan and not much in the meaning of the words. His middle section, so far as there is one, comes so early on and is so skimped

*The complete words of the Mass are given in Latin and English in Chapters 4–8.

that one is barely conscious of it. Only 12 has a Kyrie that suggests heart-felt prayer throughout and a marvellous movement it is, full of a sort of mysticism, but only twelve of the 130 bars are devoted to the words 'Christe eleison'. More often Haydn writes an almost symphonic first movement, a short slow introduction leading to a long animated Allegro; he may have got this plan from Mozart's *Coronation* Mass, K.317. Like other composers he seems to have considered the feeling behind the prayer to be so imprecisely defined that almost any emotional response was permissible. Haydn's Kyries range from excessive good humour in 7* to frightened desperation in 9, a work strongly affected by wartime conditions. Such Kyries made no impression on Beethoven who surely gave more thought to the one in Hummel's Mass in B flat with its mood of gentle pleading and roughly tripartite structure.

Gloria

According to the Roman Missal the priest should intone the opening words to a fragment of traditional plainsong, the choir coming in with 'et in terra pax', but in most Viennese Masses and in all Eisenstadt examples the opening words are sung by the choir. Conventionally the Viennese Gloria is in three main sections, fast—slow—fast.

Fast: Gloria in excelsis Deo, etc.
Slow: Qui tollis peccata mundi, etc.; in a contrasting key and usually in three-four time[7]
Fast: Quoniam tu solus sanctus, etc.

In 9, Haydn based the start of his third section on the same music as the first. Mozart had sometimes aimed at a ternary structure, most strikingly in his *Coronation* Mass, and it is hinted at in Haydn 7, in Hummel's E flat and B flat Masses and in the Missa Solemnis.

With the coming of the *galant* or early classical style around 1750 the all-pervading counterpoint of the Baroque period had

---

*The opening Largo is deeply expressive but the main Allegro, though very enjoyable as music, seems quite unrelated to the words.

fallen from favour in the Mass as in other kinds of music, except that the fugue, often at its most elaborate, retained its place at the end of the Gloria or the Credo or both. The contrast of styles that resulted could be extreme. An early example, though not in a Mass, can be found in C.P.E. Bach's Magnificat (c.1748) which is unrelievedly homophonic except for the final fugue which is enormously long and burdened with every imaginable contrapuntal ingenuity. In 1806–07 Beethoven's interest in the fugue was slight, and the one at the end of the Gloria in his Mass in C is not fully developed. You feel he wrote it only because there was a fugue at this point in his models, for instance Haydn 8, 9 and 12, and Hummel's Masses in E flat and B flat. But by the time he came to write the Missa Solemnis Beethoven's attitude to fugues was quite different. They obsessed him, and he obviously welcomed the chance to write one at the end of both Gloria and Credo.

Credo

Again the Roman Missal directs that the opening words, 'Credo in unum Deum', shall be intoned by the priest, and they are never set in Masses of the Palestrina period or indeed in liturgical examples of our own time.* But in the great Viennese period composers seldom took any notice of this directive.

Like the Gloria, the Viennese Credo was almost always in three sections:

Fast: Credo in unum Deum, etc.
Slow: Et incarnatus est, etc.; in a contrasting key
Fast: Et resurrexit tertia die, etc.

Often the Credo ended with a fugue to the words 'et vitam venturi saeculi. Amen' (and the life of the world to come, Amen) and this might be in an even faster tempo than the 'Et resurrexit'. Exceptions can be found. For instance, in his *Coronation* Mass Mozart recapped music from his first section in his third, and in his B flat Mass Hummel managed the entire Credo without any change of tempo or key signature. Beethoven was content to

*See for instance the short Mass by Stravinsky.

write in the usual three main sections and to end conventionally with a fugue as Haydn had done in 7, 8, 10, etc.

Sanctus and Benedictus

Sanctus, sanctus, sanctus, Dominus Deus Sabaoth
Pleni sunt coeli et terra gloria tua
Osanna in excelsis

Benedictus qui venit in nomine Domini,
Osanna in excelsis

All the words have been given above, and the spacing is intended to show that there are two separate sections in this movement. Indeed the rubric of the Roman Missal actually states that the Sanctus and the Benedictus must be separate because in between them the Host is elevated by the priest and 'the choir adores with the rest'. Nevertheless the gap is unlikely to exceed a minute, and in concert performances of any Mass the Sanctus and Benedictus are always sung as though they belonged to each other. In the Missa Solemnis Beethoven broke with tradition and linked them together. This had not been done before though it was not unknown for organists to improvise through the gap.

It will be noticed that the Sanctus and Benedictus both end with the same three words, 'Osanna in excelsis', and this is another unifying factor. At least it can be, but a composer may have other considerations on his mind. With both Sanctus and Benedictus being slow* and another slow movement, the Agnus Dei, coming next, composers have often felt that there were powerful reasons for varying both key and mood in this area of the Mass. But if the Benedictus is in a different key from the Sanctus,† and it often is, then the 'Osanna' at the end will have to be re-set if this different key is to be preserved, in which case the unifying factor disappears. This is what happens in the Missa Solemnis, as also in Haydn 8 and 10. Alternatively the Benedictus can end with the tonality suddenly and at the last moment

---

*Haydn 12 has a Benedictus of irresistible cheerfulness marked Molto Allegro but this Mass is eccentric in a number of ways.
†or has a different time signature. Haydn did not repeat the first 'Osanna' in 7 perhaps because he had written his Benedictus in six-eight.

disturbed so that the original 'Osanna' can be repeated, and this is what happens in Haydn 9, Hummel's Mass in E flat and Beethoven's in C. It is seldom a happy solution because the Church always wanted the first 'Osanna' to be short in order not to delay the Elevation of the Host whereas the Viennese Benedictus was nearly always of considerable length. A short 'Osanna' in a new key after a long Benedictus can sound, literally, inconclusive, as I think it does in Beethoven's Mass in C.

Agnus Dei

Agnus Dei, qui tollis peccata mundi, miserere nobis
Agnus Dei, qui tollis peccata mundi, dona nobis pacem

Like the 'Qui tollis' in the Gloria, the Agnus Dei usually begins in three-four time because this best suits the words.[8] It is also the section of the Mass that is most likely to be in a minor key and the tempo is invariably slow. In order to end on a more hopeful note it was usual in Beethoven's time to make a separate section out of the last three words, 'Dona nobis pacem', and at this point composers usually moved into the tonic major, but their reactions to these words have been almost as varied as their reactions to the Kyrie. When Haydn began writing his late Masses a desire for peace was more intense than usual because of the war that was then raging in Central Europe and in 7 he suggested this war almost operatically with drum rolls and trumpet calls that were eventually to have a profound effect on the Missa Solemnis. In 1802 the Peace of Amiens was signed; it had been foreseen the previous year. Though in fact war soon started up again, Haydn makes clear in the 'Dona nobis pacem' of 11 and 12 that he thought it was over; triumphant trumpets and drums very positively proclaim God's answer to prayer. This approach had the advantage of providing the sort of cheerful ending people expected in symphonies and concertos; they were sent home happy. In this way Haydn avoided the danger of anticlimax, a danger that is inherent in the words because they seem to insist on a quiet ending. In fact Haydn never did end his Masses quietly, but Hummel did in his B flat Mass and so did Beethoven in his C major. In both cases good writing ensures success. A quiet ending is always likely to succeed in short Masses such as those by Stravinsky and Britten, but may not in a long one, and we shall see later that Ethel Smyth was especially conscious of the problem, as perhaps was Beethoven in the Missa Solemnis.

Just as there were conventions for key contrasts in symphonies and chamber works, so there were conventions for key contrasts in Masses. Needless to say these were sometimes ignored. Weber, who had no more experience of church music than Beethoven, ignored them to such an extent in the two Masses he wrote in 1818 and 1819 that one suspects he had never found out what they were. But Beethoven was aware of them from his studying of earlier Eisenstadt Masses. The first four movements—Kyrie, Gloria, Credo and Sanctus—were almost always in the tonic, with the slow sections in the middle of the Gloria and Credo in some contrasted key. The tonic was usually abandoned for most of the Agnus Dei and restored at the 'Dona nobis pacem'. The scheme was extremely lop-sided, with the tonic dominating for more than three-quarters of the Mass (which is too long) and often not returning until the Dona (which is too late). In his Mass in C Beethoven improved on this scheme by moving away from the tonic as early as the Sanctus, and in the Missa Solemnis he moved away earlier still—for the Credo. Of his models or possible models only Cherubini had been adventurous in this way. In his last years Beethoven preferred to move to the key a third above or below the tonic rather than to the conventional sub-dominant or dominant; in his C major Mass the Sanctus is in A.* It is our loss that we no longer notice such key contrasts with pleasurable surprise.

---

*Perhaps Beethoven remembered that in Haydn's C major *Missa in tempore belli* (7) the middle section of the Gloria is in A major.

2

The Missa Solemnis Composed and Performed

The Missa Solemnis* would not have been written but for an extraordinary friendship. The Archduke Rudolph (1788–1831) was the youngest son of the Emperor Leopold II, and for most of his life his half-brother, Franz, was the ruler of the vast Austrian Empire which then included what we now know as Czechoslovakia, Hungary, Jugoslavia and Northern Italy. He was an improbable friend for a composer of modest birth, but music obsessed him as it did, to a lesser extent, so many of the Hapsburgs. When he was sixteen Beethoven began giving him piano lessons. He must already have been an accomplished pianist for almost at once Beethoven composed for him the Triple Concerto; he tactfully made the piano part slightly easier than the parts for solo violin and solo cello which were to be played by members of the Archduke's musical establishment, but it is still difficult. Over the next twenty years Beethoven presented the Archduke with virtually all his publications as well as a number of manuscripts, and he dedicated to him as many as nine masterpieces:

Piano Concerto No.4 in G, Op.58
Piano Concerto No.5 in E flat, Op.73
Piano Sonata in E flat, *Les Adieux*, Op.81
Fidelio (only the vocal score)
Violin Sonata in G, Op.96
Piano Trio in B flat, Op.97
Piano Sonata in B flat, *Hammerklavier*, Op.106
Missa Solemnis, Op.123
Grosse Fuge for string quartet, Op.133[1]

Of these works only the Piano Trio is known as *The Archduke*, and then only in Britain and America. Rudolph and the French

*The Novello vocal score spells it Missa Solennis. Sollemnis is also possible.

violinist Rode gave the first known performance of the G major Violin Sonata at one of Prince Lobkowitz's evening concerts, and though it is unlikely that Rudolph made much of the *Hammerklavier* (who could in those days?) he certainly played a large number of Beethoven's compositions up to near-professional standards. He also composed, though less professionally. He achieved a sonata for clarinet and piano, and when Beethoven sent him a four-bar theme, 'O Hoffnung', the Archduke wrote forty variations on it for piano, and Beethoven was active in getting these variations published. Rudolph was a very unusual Archduke.*

Naturally Beethoven counted on a financial return, and the Archduke was well aware of his responsibilities in this respect. In 1809, when he was no more than twenty-one, he, Prince Kinsky and Prince Lobkowitz arranged to give Beethoven an annual allowance, and as Beethoven was becoming increasingly deaf and less and less able to earn money as a performer the allowance was essential for his continuing activity as a composer. Dozens of letters from Beethoven to the Archduke survive and some from the Archduke to Beethoven, and their correspondence shows more signs of friendliness than one would expect at a period when social classes were sharply divided. Because Beethoven knew he depended on the Archduke for his bread and butter some of his sentences have a rather servile tone, but much of their correspondence is remarkable for its man-to-man flavour.

In the years 1813–17 Beethoven composed fewer masterpieces than in any other five-year period of his adult life, his time and energy being taken up with legal battles over his orphaned nephew, Karl. His affection for Karl was obsessive, and it has recently been suggested that it had sexual undertones. Schindler thought it necessary after Beethoven's death to destroy two of the Conversation Books in which Karl had recorded his side of conversations with his deaf uncle. It may be that to a lesser degree Beethoven felt a somewhat similar affection for the Archduke, a plump delicate young man who never seems to have shown any interest in the opposite sex. The affection, such as it was, was certainly reciprocated, and it was kept alive by the piano lessons Beethoven continued to give even during the composing of the Missa Solemnis. I am not for a moment suggesting

*A record of his trio for clarinet, cello and piano was issued in 1978 (CRD 1045).

impropriety nor implying any moral judgement, but this close friendship deserves a mention for without it the Missa Solemnis would not have been written.

On 24 April 1819 a very surprising event took place. It was publicly announced that Pope Pius VII had created Rudolph a Cardinal of the Roman Catholic Church, and six weeks later, on 4 June, it was announced that he was to be made Archbishop of Olmütz (now Olomouc), a city in the middle of Moravia and thus of modern Czechoslovakia. Rudolph's installation was arranged for 9 March 1820, this being the day set aside for honouring Moravia's patron saints, Cyrillus and Methodius. Beethoven was delighted by the news, and in June 1819 he wrote at length to the Archduke to congratulate him. He enclosed copies of the late cello sonatas which had just been published; also the first two movements of the *Hammerklavier* Sonata in manuscript, explaining that he had written the latter the previous year and that Rudolph would get the whole work on publication. The letter included the following sentence, the first known reference to the Missa Solemnis: 'The day on which a High Mass composed by me will be performed during the ceremonies solemnized for Your Imperial Highness will be the most glorious day of my life; and God will enlighten me so that my poor talents may contribute to the glorification of that solemn day.'[2]

The subject is introduced out of the blue, and it seems certain that Beethoven and the Archduke had discussed it before the official announcement, for the earliest of Beethoven's sketches for the Kyrie were written in the first three months of the year. Rudolph must have known of the appointment in advance and he must have told Beethoven of it. One would suppose that Rudolph himself suggested the composing of a celebratory Mass, a Mass that would bring together his two secret lives of music and religion, were it not that Schindler specifically stated that the Mass was written 'without invitation of any kind'.[3] But Schindler was not always reliable. If the idea did indeed come from Beethoven, Rudolph did not discourage him. Perhaps the end of the letter quoted above implies that religious problems were also discussed. The two men continued to meet, and not only for piano lessons; on 29 July Beethoven sent the future Archbishop three poems and suggested that he should set one of them.

There was never the slightest chance that Beethoven would

finish the Mass in time. By now he was incurably optimistic about completion dates, deceiving himself almost as often as he deceived others. Furthermore, the years when his creative urge had lain more or less fallow had been followed by a period of hardly believable activity in several areas at once. The *Hammerklavier* Sonata seems to have acted as a liberator. But Beethoven could not hope to complete the Mass when at the same time he was trying to compose a symphony, perhaps two, which he had long promised to the Philharmonic Society of London, and when he was also being attacked by an uncontrollable urge to write more sonatas for solo piano. The chaos in his workroom must have been stifling, with bits of manuscript paper lying everywhere—rough sketches, more fully composed passages, and music that he regarded as finished until he found himself rewriting it. He must have been constantly unable to find what he wanted. To make matters worse he was by this time an obsessive mover, always expecting his next lodgings to be more comfortable than the last. For instance, in November 1821 he moved to the second floor of No.222 Landstrasse in Vienna; early next May he moved to Oberdöbling, Allegasse; on 1 September he went to Baden for the sake of his health; in the middle of October he moved back to Vienna. These twelve months were not exceptional; they were typical, and he changed his servants at least as often as his lodgings. Throughout this period he was always sketching and composing several works at once. Did he take all his sketches with him every time he moved? How often did he come near to completing a movement and then lose for ever what he had scribbled of it? The astonishing thing is that in the course of some six years he got so many major works finished, even though he was three years late with the Missa Solemnis and later still with the Ninth Symphony.

I have tried to draw up a rough time-table of achievement:

1817   Little accomplished. In July Beethoven wrote to the Philharmonic Society of London to tell them that the two symphonies they had commissioned would be ready without fail by the following January. He started to sketch one in D minor but soon turned instead to a long piano sonata.

1818   He virtually completed the *Hammerklavier* Sonata,
       Op.106.

1819   The lawsuit over his nephew Karl continued to take up
       much of Beethoven's time, yet he was composing freely
       again. Schindler reported that he had never seen him in
       such a state of creative ecstasy. Early in the year he
       sketched the Kyrie of the Missa Solemnis and towards
       the end of it the Gloria; in between it was announced
       that Rudolph was to be Archbishop of Olmütz. Commis-
       sioned to write one variation for piano on a Waltz by
       Diabelli, Beethoven wrote at least four and planned
       more.

1820   In the first three months he made sketches for the Credo
       of the Missa Solemnis, but then offered to write a set of
       three piano sonatas for one of his publishers, Schlesinger
       (see letter of 30.4.20). He completed the one in E, Op.109.
       By the end of the year he had roughed out the whole of
       the Credo and was beginning to tinker with the Benedictus
       and Agnus Dei.

1821   He continued working on the Missa Solemnis. Sketches
       for the Agnus Dei are muddled up with those for his last
       two piano sonatas; he finished the A flat, Op.110, on
       Christmas Day.

1822   In the middle of January he finished the C minor Piano
       Sonata, Op.111, having composed most of it the previous
       year. By the spring he had the whole of the Missa
       Solemnis roughed out; as Thayer put it (p.813) the Mass
       was 'several times completed but never complete so long
       as it was within reach'. Beethoven returned to the *Diabelli*
       Variations and, in September, wrote the Overture, *Con-
       secration of the House*, Op.124. He was increasingly
       thinking about the Ninth Symphony.

1823   He finished the *Diabelli* Variations. In March he pre-
       sented the Archbishop with a beautifully bound copy of
       the Missa Solemnis but continued to make minor alter-
       ations. His main work this year was on the Ninth
       Symphony.

1824   He finished the Ninth Symphony in February, and on 7
       May it had its first performance together with three
       movements from the Missa Solemnis. A month earlier the

Missa Solemnis, or some of it, had been performed for the first time anywhere in St Petersburg.

These bare facts need some filling-out. It looks as though Beethoven slowed down on the Missa Solemnis as soon as he realized there was no hope of his finishing it in time for Rudolph's installation as Archbishop. On 10 November 1819 he had written to his one-time pupil, Ferdinand Ries, who was working in London, and mentioned that he had 'almost finished a new grand Mass'. He must have known this was not true and it is hard to find a reason for his misleading Ries on the subject. He was soon making similar remarks to a number of publishers, trying to set them off against each other in a way they inevitably found unendearing. Thus on 10 February 1820 he wrote to Simrock, listed various compositions he was prepared to send him, and added: 'As for the Mass which will soon be performed the fee is 125 louis d'or—it is a big work.' At the time he had done no more than rough out the first two movements and make preliminary sketches for the third. He wrote again to Simrock just over a year later, on 14 March 1821: 'You will most probably receive the Mass at Frankfurt in the middle of April.' This was a bare four weeks ahead, and it must have suddenly struck Beethoven that perhaps he was being a bit optimistic for he added a footnote: 'or at the end of April at the latest'.[4] On 13 November he offered the Mass to Schlesinger of Berlin who was publishing some of his Scotch Song arrangements as well as the three piano sonatas, and on 5 June 1822 to Peters of Leipzig ('the *greatest* work I have composed so far... several publishers have made offers for it'), and on 22 August to Artaria of Vienna—rather reluctantly in the latter case because he owed Artaria money. For one reason or another nothing came of any of these feelers. As we have seen, publishers were never enthusiastic about publishing Masses because they did not sell.

Early in 1823 Beethoven approached Diabelli who, as well as having composed the waltz on which Beethoven was writing variations (and a great many other works), ran a publishing house in Vienna. In March Schindler wrote in a Conversation Book: 'Diabelli called me today while I was passing and said he would take the Mass and publish it in two months by subscription. He guarantees you the 1000 florins—as he says he's already told

you. You can have as many copies as you want.'⁵ This was a
good offer but by now Beethoven's thoughts were running on
quite different lines. He had just had a copy of the Missa
Solemnis made for the Archbishop and he had presented it to
him in person; he probably received a monetary gift in return.
It then occurred to him that it might be a good idea to have more
copies made and to offer them to Crowned Heads of Europe at
50 ducats each. Because he thought they might feel affronted if
publication followed too hard on their paying for their copies, he
decided to postpone publication. Naturally Diabelli was furious.
Among those who agreed to pay for manuscript scores were the
Czar of Russia, the Kings of Prussia, Saxony, France and
Denmark, Prince Nikolas Galitzin of Russia and Prince Anton
Radziwill of Poland. Beethoven did not offer a copy to George
IV because, when Prince Regent, he had not bothered either to
acknowledge or to pay for the score of *Wellington's Victory* which
Beethoven had expectantly sent him. Louis XVIII not only paid
for his score but sent Beethoven as a bonus a gold medal weighing
22 louis d'or. One of the copies sent to Russia made possible the
first performance anywhere of the Mass on 7 April 1824.

It might be thought that the score sent to Prince Galitzin had
this unexpected result and probably it did; as we shall see, he
wrote to Beethoven immediately after the concert to congratulate
him on the music. But years later he wrote to Schindler with
strange waspishness: 'Who acted more nobly, Beethoven or I?
He sends me without warning a useless score for which I had
not asked. He then makes me pay fifty ducats for it when I could
have bought a printed copy a few months later for only five
thalers.'

While these copies were being made it was suggested to Beethoven that he should compose another Mass, this time for the
Austrian Emperor. The Court composer, Anton Tayber, had just
died, and Beethoven's friend and patron, Count Moritz Lichnowsky, thought he might get the job if he wrote a Mass to the
Emperor's liking and requirements; this meant that it should be
mainly for chorus with short simple solos for a boy treble and
a boy alto and no tenor or bass soloists. As for the orchestra,
solos for violin, oboe and clarinet would be acceptable. 'His
Majesty likes to have fugues well worked out but not too long;
the Sanctus and Osanna as short as possible in order not to delay

the Transubstantiation.'[6] In fact Beethoven had already been considering another Mass. One of his notebooks mentions 'A Kyrie in the second Mass with wind instruments and organ only', and a sketch for a Dona nobis pacem entitled 'Mass in C sharp minor' was presumably intended for the same work. One wonders if the fugue at the start of the C sharp minor string quartet, or something like it, can have been originally intended for this work. The Count may have expected Beethoven to lay everything else aside and jump at this chance of putting his chaotic financial affairs in order, but Beethoven wrote to everyone concerned to say he was too busy to write a Mass for the Emperor. Schindler thought that his main reason for refusing was that he did not want to become a court servant and lose his freedom. 'His guiding principle, "Liberty ennobles the soul and exalts the spirit", had wavered for a time but was again firm and resolute.'[7]

In 1822 Beethoven and his brother Johann patched up a long-standing quarrel, and on 8 September Beethoven wrote to him in the unbuttoned way he kept for close friends and relatives: 'Two women singers called on us today, and as they absolutely insisted on being allowed to kiss my hands and as they were decidedly pretty, I preferred to offer them my mouth to kiss.' Almost certainly they were the soprano Henriette Sontag and the contralto Karoline Unger who were then only sixteen and nineteen respectively. They had probably been told that Beethoven was writing large-scale vocal works and they called with an eye to the main chance. He did not forget them.

Early in 1824 several of Beethoven's friends began trying to arrange a concert in which both the Ninth Symphony and the Missa Solemnis would be heard in Vienna for the first time. Prince Lichnowsky, the violinist Schuppanzigh and Schindler all did their best to make the complex arrangements that were necessary, much hindered by Beethoven's deafness and chronic suspicion that everyone had underhand motives for what they recommended. Though the Conversation Books do not record Beethoven's answers to what they said, these can often be guessed easily enough. He had strong views and gripped on to them tightly. He wanted Sontag and Unger for the women soloists though Schindler, who thought they were younger than they really were (eighteen and twenty-one by this time), maintained that their voices were insufficiently matured and not strong enough. Beethoven's wishes prevailed, and as both girls won fame all over Western Europe soon afterwards his reasons may have been more solidly based than one might suspect.

The concert was originally to have been given in the Theater-an-der-Wien. The director, Count Palffy, offered his house on very generous terms and his orchestra for nothing. Beethoven was agreeable to this arrangement provided that his friend Schuppanzigh led the orchestra. Everyone told him that there were bound to be objections to this unless he wrote a very tactful letter to Clement, the leader of the theatre band, but so far as is known Beethoven never did. Prince Lichnowsky agreed that the orchestra should be doubled (he presumably meant the wind players) but pleaded for the avoidance of unnecessary expense. The theatre chorus, though good, was also thought to be too small; it was realized that competent extras would not be easily found. All these plans went by the board when Clement refused to give up his position to Schuppanzigh and was backed by the entire orchestra.

There was nothing for it but to turn down Palffy's offer and at much greater expense book the Court Theatre together with its orchestra and chorus. With 46 strings[8] and doubled wind the orchestra must have numbered over 70, and it was clear to everyone but Beethoven that there was no chance of his making much money out of the venture. When, after the concert, he heard how little he had made, he wept.

The performance of a solemn Mass in a public theatre was vigorously opposed by the church authorities in Vienna, and though Prince Lichnowsky knew all the right people and could pull strings he was able to get permission for the concert only on the undertaking that the Latin words of the Mass were not sung. There were worse difficulties to come. Those who arranged this concert would have given the music little more than a casual glance; there seemed no reason to do more. Symphonies could be expected to play for about 40 minutes and Masses for about 45. When it was realized that Beethoven's symphony and Mass were both double length and of unprecedented difficulty, it became clear that the programme was far too ambitious, and it was agreed to give only three movements of the Missa Solemnis, the Kyrie, Credo and Agnus Dei. They were to be billed as Three Grand Hymns and sung to innocuous German words which almost totally concealed Beethoven's musical intentions.

There was endless trouble over the copying. Schlemmer, the only copyist in Vienna who could accurately decipher Beethoven's appalling writing, had just died, and none of the five substitutes came up to the composer's exacting standards. Not only could they not read what he had written, their own writing was often faulty into the bargain. He wrote to one of them as follows: 'Do use your intelligence sometimes. . . Half your notes are neither exactly on the lines nor exactly on the spaces. If all the movements of the symphony are to be copied as you have copied the first Allegro the whole thing will be useless.'[9] Most composers are on edge before important first performances, but Beethoven's tetchiness exceeded all reason. The following are brief, undated notes he scribbled a week or two before the concert, and only the saintly patience of his friends kept them on speaking terms with him. To Schuppanzigh: 'Don't visit me any more; I am not giving a concert.' To Schindler: 'I feel cooked, stewed and roasted. What on earth is to be the outcome of this much discussed concert if the prices are not raised? What will be left for me after such heavy expenses? Look what the copying alone is costing.' He also sent a one-line note to Schindler that was almost the same as the one he had sent Schuppanzigh; Prince Lichnowsky's version had the addition of a veiled and unexplained insult: 'I despise what is false. Don't visit me any more. There will be no concert.'

But there was. Beethoven's friends refused to be discouraged. Chorus rehearsals got underway; Schuppanzigh rehearsed the strings; the soloists came to Beethoven's lodgings with Ignaz Umlauf who was to direct the concert. Now in his forties, Umlauf was in charge of the operas at the Court Theatre; he had indeed directed the revivals of *Fidelio* in both 1814 and 1822, and Beethoven felt a good deal of respect for him. The tenor soloist was Anton Haizinger who had just sung Florestan in *Fidelio* and the bass soloist was originally to have been one Preisinger, but after a try-out it was realized that he would never surmount the music's difficulties and he was replaced by Josef Seipelt. Haizinger was a young man with a light-weight voice; Seipelt was much older and had a slightly nasal tone. All the soloists complained that their parts were too difficult, and the girls complained particularly of all the high notes, as well they might, but Beethov-

en would not alter them. Karoline Unger was moved to declare
that he was a tyrant over all their vocal organs; which he may
or may not have heard.

The concert began with the Overture, *Consecration of the
House*, and because the rest of the programme was being given
with double woodwind, extra parts had to be copied which all
added to the concert's expense. No doubt this went well enough
but in the two first performances standards must have been
deplorable. Only two full rehearsals had been possible for this
appallingly difficult programme because the Court Theatre
orchestra had its other commitments. All copyists make mistakes
and on this occasion, Beethoven's writing being what it was, they
must have made more than usual, yet there can have been little
or no time to make corrections. In any case at final rehearsals it
is up to the composer to point out mistakes, and this composer
could not hear if the notes were right or wrong. The director of
the chorus told him that his sopranos were quite incapable of
singing the fugal entry in the Credo which begins with four high
B flat minims, but again Beethoven would alter nothing. As
Schindler wrote later, the result was that the singers 'made their
own simplifications. When the sopranos could not reach the high
notes as written, they simply did not sing. Anyway the composer,
although he was standing in the middle of the ensemble, could
hear nothing of what was going on.'[10] As for the tempi, Umlauf
told everyone on the quiet to pay no attention to any arm
movements Beethoven might make but to look at him; which in
fact is what he had told the singers and orchestra back in 1814
when he was directing the revival of *Fidelio*.

Beethoven was not aware of the imperfections. After the final
rehearsal he stood at the door and charmingly embraced all the
amateur performers as they came out. But the imperfections must
have been obvious enough to the more musical of those who
attended the concert itself. Furthermore, besides being very
difficult for the performers, the two new works were also very
difficult to understand. Nevertheless, many people found the
occasion extremely exciting. Beethoven was greatly respected in
Vienna and his famous deafness must have added to the emotional
impact of the occasion. The sight of his short stumpy figure
among the players and his obvious inability to hear his own
music made everyone desperately anxious that the occasion should

be a success, especially as it might well prove to be his last public appearance. He received tumultuous applause, of which he was quite unaware until Karoline Unger turned him round so that he could see the clapping hands.

Yet disillusion set in almost as soon as the concert was over. The Missa Solemnis seemed to have no future. Rudolph had not been present, pleading that he could not leave Olmütz, but almost certainly he felt that an Archbishop should not be seen in a theatre listening to a Credo even when it was sung to inoffensive German words. As Beethoven must have realized, if his Missa Solemnis could not be performed with the proper Latin words in a public theatre it would hardly ever be performed at all as he intended, and indeed it was to be a sadly neglected masterpiece for many years to come. Worst of all for Beethoven was the paltry financial return for so many years of hard work. He felt someone must be to blame for this, so he wrote to the wretched Schindler:

I do not accuse you of having done anything wicked in connexion with the concert. But stupidity and arbitrary behaviour have ruined many an undertaking... Stopped up sluices often overflow quite suddenly... I must confess that your presence irritates me in a great many ways... I have found you out once already in a way that was *unfavourable to you*, and *so have other people*.[11]

It is much to Schindler's credit that he did not destroy this monstrous letter.

However, only a day or so later, on 12 May, Beethoven wrote in his sunniest vein to 'My lovely and precious Sontag'.

I've kept meaning to call on you sometime and thank you for your fine contribution to my concert. Well, in a day or two I hope to visit you and take you and Unger out to lunch in the Prater or the Augarten, for this is the most beautiful time of year for that sort of thing.

One hopes the day turned out as Beethoven wished and that the girls enjoyed themselves too.

But none of them will have much enjoyed a repeat of the concert on 23 May in the Redoutensaal. The day was warm and sunny and very few people came. The Ninth Symphony was played complete but of the Mass only the easiest movement was performed, the Kyrie.

The Vienna performances had been forestalled, it will be remembered, by one in St Petersburg on 7 April, and in spite of the waspishness he displayed later on the subject it is supposed that the driving force behind this performance was Prince Nikolas Galitzin. About thirty years old, he was an industrious promoter of musical events in St Petersburg as well as an amateur cellist of some ability. But musical standards in Russia cannot have been as high as those in Central Europe, and both choir and orchestra must have found the problems of the Credo insuperable. The letter of thanks and congratulation that the Prince wrote to Beethoven the day after the concert included the ominous sentence: 'Your genius is centuries before its time.'[12] Though he praised with ecstasy the Kyrie and Gloria, and considered that 'the masterly harmony and the moving melody of the Benedictus transport the heart to a plane that is truly blissful', he made no mention of the Credo and the probability is that it was omitted. He also reveals that Prince Radziwill who had just arrived from Berlin attended the performance, and that 'he had not known' the music before; presumably he had not looked at the copy of the score which he too had received and paid for.

The Missa Solemnis was repeated in St Petersburg the following year.

Both the Mass and the Ninth Symphony were published by Schott of Mainz. They happened to have written to Beethoven about something else and in reply, on 10 March 1824 (two months before the first performance), he offered them both works as also a string quartet. At first they stalled, thinking his price too high, but agreement was reached and the full score of the Ninth Symphony appeared in August 1826 and of the Mass in the spring of 1827, just after Beethoven's death. The other publishers with whom he had negotiated cannot have been best pleased.

3
Beethoven as a Christian

No one would dispute that Beethoven was sincere when he wrote the Missa Solemnis; the sincerity of great music is *sui generis*. But with a large-scale religious work there is the question of whether its sincerity derives in part from the composer's religious beliefs, and if you think it does then you must also think that what he believes makes a difference, that it matters from the music's point of view. It appears to have made a difference in the *St Matthew Passion* and *Messiah*, or so many people would think. On the other hand some would argue that Berlioz's *Te Deum*, magnificent though it is, lacks the final crown of religious sincerity, to its disadvantage.

The views of critics on how far, if at all, Beethoven's beliefs affected the Missa Solemnis have been very varied. Thayer maintained that 'poetical, not to say dramatic elements were those he most wanted to delineate' rather than the great Christian truths, but Tovey thought it 'a mistake to regard Beethoven as composing his text in any agnostic spirit of art for art's sake', and Alec Robertson, himself a convinced Catholic, wrote that 'the liturgical text was not, to Beethoven, just an excuse for music but the fountain and origin of his inspiration'.[1] Such uncertainty about Beethoven's beliefs and their musical implications is reason enough for a brief interlude on the subject.

Beethoven was a thinking man, more philosophically inclined than most of the great composers, and I am conscious of presumption in trying to encapsulate his beliefs in one short chapter, especially as he himself hardly ever talked about them. 'Beethoven', wrote Schindler,

was brought up in the Roman Catholic religion. His entire life is proof that he was truly religious at heart . . . One of his marked characteristics was that he never discussed religious subjects or the dogmas of the

various Christian Churches. We can, however, say almost certainly that
his religious views were not so much based on church doctrine as on
a sort of deism.[2]

His reading included both the old Greek philosophers such as
Aristotle and modern writers on Oriental religions, and on 2
November 1809, 'after suffering every hardship that one could
conceivably endure' as a result of Napoleon's assault on Vienna,
he was led to write of his philosophy with quite uncharacteristic
candour—to his publishers, Breitkopf & Härtel, of all people:

There is hardly any treatise which could be too learned *for me*. I have
not the slightest pretension to what is properly called erudition, yet
from childhood I have striven to understand what *the better and wiser
people* of every age were driving at in their works. Shame on an artist
who does not consider it his duty to achieve at least as much.

He became increasingly interested in recent translations of Per-
sian literature transcribed by Herder and Hammer, and about
1810 he himself took the trouble to transcribe a number of
passages, among them this one:

God is immaterial; since he is invisible he can have no form, but from
what we observe in his works we may conclude that he is eternal,
omnipotent, omniscient and omnipresent—The mighty one is he who
is free from all desire; he alone; there is no greater than he. Brahma;
his spirit is enwrapped in himself... Thou alone art the truly blessed
one (Bhagavan); thou, the essence of all laws, the image of all wisdom,
present throughout the universe, thou upholdest all things. Sun, ether,
Brahmah. [These three words are crossed out.][3]

Beethoven was clearly interested in what today would be called
Comparative Religion.

He read with special interest an essay by Schiller, *Die Sendung
Moses*, much of which is about the nature of Egyptian wisdom,
and he copied out three aphorisms which, according to Schiller,
had been found 'under an ancient monument of Isis' and 'upon
a pyramid at Sais':

I am that which is.

I am everything that is, that was, and that will be; no mortal man has
raised my veil.

He is of himself alone, and it is to this aloneness that all things owe their being.

Beethoven had these aphorisms framed under glass so that he could keep them in view on his work desk. They later passed to Schindler.[4]

There can be little doubt that in his twenties and thirties Beethoven turned against the Christian faith as the sole guardian of truth, or that in his forties he rather hesitantly returned to it in a form modified to suit himself. The return may well have owed much to his friendship with the Archduke Rudolph, who must have been obsessed with ecclesiastical ambition at least by 1816. During the piano lessons Beethoven occasionally gave him, the conversation must surely have switched now and then from musical to religious problems. On 1 September 1817 Beethoven wrote to him on the subject of the ill-health from which both had recently been suffering, and the end of this letter is strikingly different from any that Beethoven had written before:

Surely God will hear my prayer and will once more liberate me from so many calamities, seeing that since my childhood I have served Him trustfully and have performed good actions wherever I could. Hence on Him alone I place my reliance and hope that in all my manifold miseries the All-Highest will not let me utterly perish.

It could be argued that Beethoven was only trying to write what he thought would please his increasingly-devout patron, but this seems unlikely. His 'manifold miseries' were caused by his recalcitrant nephew, Karl, for whom he felt responsible, as well as by ill-health, and he had recently been encouraging Karl to say his prayers at night; he even knelt down and said them with him, as Karl testified in the guardianship proceedings. Furthermore, it is hard to believe he would ever have embarked on the Missa Solemnis without some kind of religious stimulus. As he began thinking about the music in 1818 he jotted down an aide-mémoire that has chanced to survive. After advising himself to look at other settings of the Mass and other 'Christian-Catholic hymns and psalms generally' (what can they have been?) he ended: 'Tranquilly will I submit myself to all vicissitudes and place my sole confidence in Thy unalterable goodness, O God . . . Be my rock, my light, forever my trust.'[5] He is not here thinking of Brahma, nor is he writing to please the Archduke; he is sincerely asking for God's help in the enormous task he has set himself.

A Christian of sorts, but not a conventional one; it is unlikely that in his later years Beethoven ever went to church. It is also unlikely that he ever believed in all the details of Catholic doctrine. Schubert when setting the Mass would leave out phrases in the Credo which he could not stomach. Writing for an Archbishop Beethoven could hardly have done the same but it may be significant that, as we shall see later, he went out of his way to make certain phrases in his own Credo inaudible.

Charles Rosen considers that both the Beethoven Masses are 'frankly concert pieces, and more effective outside than inside a church', but Alec Robertson thought the Missa Solemnis 'ill-suited to the concert-hall, and only really at home in the large spaces of a cathedral. Those who have heard it sung in the liturgy in St Stephen's, Vienna, speak of it as an unforgettable experience.'[6] Writing just before the war, Walter Riezler expressed a more pessimistic view; the Missa Solemnis was 'never quite at home' in the concert-hall and yet 'in a church where divine office is of prime importance, full justice can never be done to its music. Thus, in common with many other great works of art, it has grown up in a realm that lies beyond the bounds of practical possibilities.' The same can be said of Bach's B minor Mass, and in neither case is such despair well-founded. Both can be overwhelming in their effect in the concert-hall. Their future in church is much more problematic.

Since the Second Vatican Council of 1962, the old objections to what was sung in the Mass have been stood on their head. No longer is it wrong for such music to sound operatic; indeed with congregations today expected to respond only to what is more or less up-to-date, the style of Massenet's operas is now a commonplace in Catholic services. The modern objection to the Missa Solemnis in a cathedral, apart from the expense of providing the orchestra, would be that the music is beyond the comprehension of many ordinary church-goers. It remains to be seen whether it will be sung more often as part of the liturgy; taking the Catholic Church as a whole, it could hardly be sung less frequently. Beethoven himself must have given thought to the problem, and one wonders what he hoped for.

4
Kyrie

Kyrie eleison,	Lord have mercy upon us,
Christe eleison,	Christ have mercy upon us,
Kyrie eleison.	Lord have mercy upon us.

No other prayer, Catholic or Protestant, achieves the basic simplicity of this one. There are only six words and three of them are the same. It is precisely because they are so simple that they can be set in so many different ways. Indeed you would hardly guess at a first hearing that the quietly reverent Kyrie in Beethoven's Mass in C sprang from the same words as the tragic and despairing Kyrie in Haydn 9. Nineteenth century composers were much more anxious than their predecessors to vary the way they began their major works, and they welcomed the chances offered by a prayer whose mood is never made clear. Mozart was prepared on occasions to begin works in the same category with the same cliché, but Beethoven's last five symphonies show an astonishing variety of openings, and it is not surprising that he launches his two Masses with music of total dissimilarity. He had an additional reason for so doing. The Mass in C had been written for performance in a comparatively small church. The Missa Solemnis was intended for a much larger building and a much grander occasion. This is a cathedral Kyrie. The great chords that punctuate it would have echoed magnificently round the high vaulted nave of Olmütz Cathedral had the music been finished in time. But Beethoven is not aiming at flamboyance. The great chords of the opening are separated by music that reflects the last words of the tempo marking, 'Mit Andacht' (with devotion). According to Tovey, Beethoven 'brings out an overwhelming and overwhelmed sense of the Divine glory, with which he invariably and immediately contrasts the nothingness of man'.[1]

Composers sometimes try to compensate for the fewness of the
Kyrie words by devising long or comparatively long melodies
with several notes to the syllable and a verbal repetition of which
one is seldom conscious because of the continuous flow of the
tune. Bach did this in his B minor Mass and so did Beethoven
in his Mass in C major. But in the Missa Solemnis he does not
shrink from building the main section of his Kyrie on a succession
of very short phrases. There is a particularly pregnant one for
the first violins in bars 3–6 which, as Walter Riezler has shown,[2]
is 'a germinal motive of the greatest fertility' (Ex.1). It keeps
recurring throughout the Missa Solemnis, and if one's first
reaction is to suspect that it keeps recurring in all other Masses
too, let me stress that it does not do so in Beethoven's earlier

Ex.1

Mass. The phrase consists of a rising fourth followed by a
stepwise descent to the starting-point, and Riezler points out that
'Palestrina's famous *Missa Papae Marcelli* has an almost identical
Leitmotiv (G-C-B-A-G)'. I think myself that this is a coincidence
and that Palestrina influenced Beethoven's harmony rather than
his melody, and even then only at widely-spaced intervals.

Two other tiny phrases occur immediately after Ex. 1:

Ex.2a   Ex.2b

The second of them is later to be sung to the word 'eleison'.
When the singers enter with a repeat of the opening bars the
chorus have *fortissimo* chords representing Tovey's 'Divine Glory'
while the soloists, one after the other, alternate with the chorus
as they express 'the nothingness of man'. When the oboe introduces a gentle pleading phrase, the second of those given above
can be heard in the middle of the harmony:

Ex.3

The two upper parts come near to committing the sin of 'consecutive octaves' (which perhaps is why the lower one is not given in my vocal score), and we shall later come on another example of Beethoven being magnificently indifferent to convention. In performance the ear detects nothing wrong, which of course is all that matters.

The oboe theme contains another device that permeates not only the Missa Solemnis but most of Beethoven's other late works as well, and that is his liking for tying notes of the same length across the barline. The device even crept into the famous choral theme of the Ninth Symphony which is otherwise quite free of any trace of sophistication:

Ex.4

The ties at the very start of the Kyrie should show us what to expect. The opening chord starts in the middle of the bar but we hear it as a first beat, and only become aware of its true nature later on. Beethoven liked to intrigue, in both senses, by denying us certainty as to what he was up to. Incidentally, that pleading oboe phrase starts with a rising fourth and very nearly returns stepwise to its starting-point.

In any Mass the most evocative words, those most likely to be many times repeated, are usually spondees; that is, they have two long syllables of which the first is accented. Such words are 'Christe', 'Credo' and 'Dona'. In the Missa Solemnis Beethoven usually sets these and many similar words to a falling third, which indeed reflects the way we say them. He had never set them in this way in his Mass in C. This falling third is a fingerprint common to all five movements of the Missa Solemnis but Beethoven used it prominently in one of his other late works as well, the *Hammerklavier* Piano Sonata. In the Mass we are first aware of this falling two-note phrase in the middle section of the Kyrie, where it is frequently sung to the word 'Christe', but Beethoven recognized the need for a more flowing theme as well:

Ex.5

The two themes occur in double counterpoint; that is, they make sense whichever one forms the bass. As Riezler pointed out, the flowing theme starts with a rising fourth which then falls stepwise, and it is thus akin to the violin theme on the first page of the Kyrie. Wind and timpani are soon filling in with the spondee rhythm associated with the word 'Christe' even when no one is singing the word. Soloists and chorus become increasingly interlocked and the scoring increasingly thick perhaps to suggest a universal pleading for mercy, the prayers rising from every quarter of the globe.

Beethoven accepts the ternary form indicated by the words, but makes the return of the opening music more symphonic than it was originally; that is, he develops the themes more positively. After no more than a dozen bars he begins to alter his material, and he is soon paying particular attention to Ex.2b. When each section of the chorus has sung the phrase in turn he achieves a climax by having it in rough *stretto*, that is, with the phrases overlapping. The music sinks to a *pianissimo*. Then comes an unforgettable peak of anguish, a *fortissimo* cry for mercy from the whole chorus and orchestra; it impresses because it arises so suddenly and unexpectedly from music that is otherwise uniformly soft. The dramatic *piano* that follows lasts almost to the end of the movement. The oboe's pleading phrase is prominent. The movement ends with the sopranos of the chorus singing very quietly that falling third that is so characteristic of the whole work. 'One of Beethoven's most beautiful quiet codas', thought Tovey, and who would disagree?

Beethoven's publishers used as their source his autograph score of the Missa Solemnis rather than any of the much neater but probably inaccurate copies that had been made. Schindler reported and deplored that even in his day the autograph had been split up and sold movement by movement, and today only the Kyrie seems to be available in photographic reproduction. It looks like what a composer might write before making his fair copy—only Beethoven never made a fair copy. Several pages are crossed out, and twice when he was dissatisfied with the right-hand half of a page he stuck a piece of manuscript paper on top and then, because it stuck out to the right, he had to fold it over. One of these occasions was the transition from the 'Kyrie eleison' to the 'Christe eleison'. Composers often find linking passages more of a bother than their actual themes; after a great deal of erasing Beethoven got this one to his satisfaction by reducing seven bars to four. He also had trouble getting back to his 'Kyrie eleison' but not nearly so much. This is a very effective transition because it manages to be both simple and unexpected. Beethoven ends his middle section very quietly in F sharp minor without a C sharp; then, before the chorus have finished singing this chord, the orchestra suddenly bursts in with the first D major chord of the movement and the chorus seems to have changed key without any change in their notes. At this point Beethoven left his manuscript blank except for the words 'come sopra' which told both copyists and printers to repeat his opening bars. The great classical composers never normally wrote out more of a recap than they had to. In the last two bars it was an afterthought and a good one to cross out the long-held doubling for the orchestra and leave the chorus virtually unaccompanied. There are literally hundreds of such alterations in the manuscript; Beethoven constantly changed his mind about details. Ink splodges are numerous; one measures roughly four inches by one and a half which is even larger than the fine example in the autograph score of the 'Amen' chorus of *Messiah*. A dreadful page from near the end of the Agnus Dei is reproduced in the Eulenburg score.

A preliminary sketch book mainly devoted to the Kyrie is now in the Wittgenstein Collection in Vienna and is thought to date from the winter of 1818–19. Another sketch book of 44 pages, small enough to slip into a pocket, is almost entirely given over to themes for the Credo and probably dates from between December 1819 and April 1820. It is now in the Beethoven-Haus in Bonn, and it has been transcribed and published by Dr Joseph Schmidt-Görg.[3]

5
Gloria

Most of the words of the Mass require music in a slow or moderately slow tempo and composers have to make the most of such opportunities as there are for contrasting speed and vigour. Apart from brief moments in the Credo and Sanctus only the Gloria calls positively for vigour, and then only at the beginning and the end. A fast-slow-fast design for the Gloria is to be found in all but the shortest Masses and it can be likened to the design of the so-called Italian Overtures of Beethoven's infancy and earlier. I shall take each of the three main sections in turn.

Gloria in excelsis Deo, et in terra pax hominibus bonae voluntatis. Laudamus te, benedicamus te, adoramus te, glorificamus te; gratias agimus tibi propter magnam gloriam tuam; Domine Deus, Rex coelestis, Deus pater omnipotens.

Glory be to God on high, and in earth peace, good will towards men. We praise thee, we bless thee, we worship thee, we glorify thee, we give thanks to thee for thy great glory, O Lord God, heavenly King, God the father Almighty.

Domine fili unigenite Jesu Christe: Domine Deus, agnus Dei, filius Patris;

O Lord, the only-begotten Son, Jesu Christ: O Lord God, Lamb of God, Son of the Father;

Beethoven set all these words in one quick section in three-four time. He slowed down slightly for 'gratias agimus tibi propter magnam gloriam tuam', presumably for musical rather than verbal reasons, and at this point he modulated into B flat, so often the contrasting key throughout the Missa Solemnis. It is arguable that from the point of view of the sense, the slow middle section should start at 'Domine fili', for the second paragraph as shown above belongs to the 'Qui tollis peccata mundi' that comes next, but Beethoven followed Viennese tradition in preserving the vigorous tempo longer than the words seem to require.

The impact of this very fast, very loud section is shattering. The main tune has been specially devised so that it can be effectively played by trumpets and horns as well as everyone else, and there is not much let-up when, at bar 5, the tune is sung by the altos of the chorus.

Ex.6

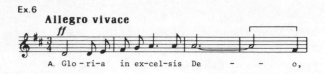

Altos are always the least assertive members of any chorus, and the fact that Beethoven chose to make them introduce the Gloria theme on their own, comparatively low in their compass, must mean that he wanted the orchestra to dominate and did not much mind if the altos' entry was barely audible. Perhaps there is a touch of symbolism here, the adulation of Man (the chorus) surfacing only gradually behind the long-established and intense adulation of the heavenly host. There must certainly be symbolism in the way the tune rises. But when each section of the chorus has struggled in turn for a hearing—significantly the most easily heard, the sopranos, come last—Beethoven unites the four groups and has each of them high in their compass for maximum penetration. He repeats the word 'gloria' much more often than is usual, and as in his Mass in C he is undecided as to its accentuation.

After 42 bars of unceasing *fortissimo* for everyone there occurs a dramatic contrast, one of the most startling of many in this highly dramatic setting. Before the echo of the last *fortissimo* note has had time to die away the basses on their own are singing 'Et in terra pax' on a low A and so softly that we are unlikely to hear what they are singing about. The accompaniment consists of little more than *pizzicato* chords. The rest of the chorus joins in with sublime lyricism but the contrast is short-lived. Brass and drums are soon blazing away with the opening tune.

After another sudden *pianissimo* for 'Adoramus te' the basses introduce the first fugal passage in the work:

The tied crotchets 'throw' the rhythm agreeably so that we momentarily lose the whereabouts of the main beats. This fugue subject is soon being worked in loose *stretto*, the entries overlapping. The music continues to be very loud but Beethoven has in view a quiet section of greater length than he has so far allowed himself in the Gloria, and for this he lets his clarinets drop out of the final bars of his *fortissimo* tutti, allowing the players some ten seconds to switch from clarinets in C to clarinets in B flat; little enough time, one might think, to change instruments, but modern players face no problem. Clarinets in C have been obsolete for a century and more, and the players will have been blowing B flat clarinets from the start of the movement, transposing their parts as they play. At much the same point Beethoven gives his first and second horns (but not the third and fourth) a similar number of bars rest to allow them to change from a D crook to an E flat, but again modern players need not hurry themselves; all the crooks they need are built into the modern valve horn and they could have managed the change of key without any rests at all.

Though the tempo is very little slower, the new key, B flat, the low dynamic, *piano*, and the emphasis on solo singers and on wind instruments together provide a welcome contrast. For the first 127 bars of this Gloria the woodwind players have been blowing away without any hope of reaching their audience, at times being inaudible even to themselves. All good composers are conscious of an obligation to make their music interesting to play as well as to hear even if in our own times some of them do very little about it, and Beethoven saw the next 30 bars or so as a chance to ingratiate himself with those members of the orchestra he had so far neglected as well as to offer his audience some delicate coloration. At first clarinets and bassoons seem to be searching for a new tune; when the first clarinet and the first horn find what is required it is immediately taken up by the tenor soloist in recognition of its supreme loveliness:

Ex.8

The other soloists join in quietly. The chorus returns with a crescendo that leads back to the original tempo and the original theme, Ex.6, this time in E flat. But the original theme will not now fit the words so Beethoven lets the orchestra play it while the chorus sings the word 'Deus' in pairs of octaves to those falling thirds which by now we almost take for granted:

Ex.9

A few bars later the evocative word 'omnipotens' causes a predictable explosion of sound. Beethoven goes so far as to mark both chorus and orchestra *fff* to show that he wanted something quite exceptional, and for the first time in the Missa Solemnis he brings in his trombones, but for six bars only. The climax falls away quickly for the very next words refer to 'the only begotten Son', and as so often (more particularly in the Mass in C) Beethoven prefers soft music for Christ and an emphasis on tunes in thirds or, less often, in sixths. Such tunes are usually stepwise in their movement; here they are played by the woodwind or sung by the soloists. This first section of the Gloria ends with yet another *fortissimo* outburst, short-lived but of tremendous effect. Woodwind and horns link this first section to the slow one in the middle of the Gloria with chords held over the double-bar between them.

Qui tollis peccata mundi, miserere nobis. Qui tollis peccata mundi, suscipe deprecationem nostram. Qui sedes ad dexteram Patris, miserere nobis.	Thou that takest away the sins of the world, have mercy upon us. Thou that takest away the sins of the world, receive our prayer. Thou that sittest at the right hand of God the Father, have mercy upon us.

Glorification now gives way to humble supplication and like most composers at this point Beethoven slows down his tempo very considerably—to a Larghetto in two-four time. There is no overall theme as there is in the two outside quick sections, and the key changes quite often. The constants are the tempo, the time signature and the emphasis on wind instruments.

It will be noticed that two phrases in the above text occur twice. On both occasions Beethoven sets the word 'tollis' to a falling third:

Ex.10

He does not relate the two settings of 'miserere nobis' but this was certainly the phrase in which he felt most interest for he repeats it over and over again to a variety of wide-ranging tunes of increasing lyrical beauty, nearly all of them sung by the soloists. None of these tunes occurs more than once in precisely the same form and the impression is given of individual utterances rather than of a corporate prayer.

Glorification returns briefly for 'Qui sedes ad dexteram Patris'. The sopranos of the chorus have their first bar of high B flats; they are to have plenty more before they are through. The outburst would have been more effective had Beethoven not taken his basses down to low F where, with the sopranos straining after those high B flats, they cannot hope to be audible. There are two or three such miscalculations in the Missa Solemnis and they remind one how long it must have been since poor Beethoven had actually heard a choral climax: It is not surprising that with his lack of experience of music's sound he should occasionally have miscalculated; what is surprising is that he miscalculated so seldom.

When he returns to 'miserere nobis' he intensifies the emotional content of the melismata he gives his soloists:

Ex. 11

But at the climax he turns to the chorus, contriving their outburst with a superb sense of the dramatic:

The mild crescendo at the start of this quotation in no way prepares us for the *fortissimo* chord. The key, F sharp minor following on F major, is completely unexpected as is the marvellously bleak six-four chord; trombones add to the impact. There is a touch of hysteria about the syncopated string writing indicated above, if we can hear it. As the climax disintegrates Beethoven feels an emotional need for extra syllables. In the quotation given above, the tenor soloist's 'o' and the chorus's 'ah' may be unliturgical but they add much to the fervency of the prayer—in an almost operatic way—as do the three-note wailing phrases in the last four bars for oboe, bassoon and lower strings. The fact that the middle note of these phrases is discordant adds to their emotional effect. At the same point in the Mass in C Beethoven had introduced rather similar wailing phrases except that the middle note is a semitone down instead of up.[1] He ends his slow section *pianissimo* and in C sharp major, whittling away the notes of the chord until only C sharp itself is left.

Quoniam tu solus sanctus, tu solus Dominus, tu solus altissimus Jesu Christe, cum sancto spiritu in gloria Dei Patris. Amen.

For thou only art Holy; thou only art the Lord; thou only, O Christ, with the Holy Ghost, art the Most High, in the glory of God the Father. Amen.

Beethoven sets these words in two sections, both marked Allegro (with qualifications). The first is quite short and in three-four time; it includes all the words set out above. The second does this too, but unobtrusively; the emphasis is entirely on the last five words which underpin an enormous fugue.

The three-four Allegro maestoso begins with a very soft timpani roll on A, and as this starts under the C sharp left over from the Larghetto we soon sense a dominant chord that is going to lead the music back to the starting key, D major. The 'Quoniam' theme features the now predictable tied crotchets and dramatic contrasts between loud and soft:

Ex.13

Who, asked to write down the first six bars of the above from the sound, would get them right? The chord progressions at the climax have a modal flavour.

The great fugue that follows[2] combines a rock-like stability with a suggestion of terrestrial adoration rising heavenwards. This last is due to its subject being based on a sequence of rising fourths as the asterisks make clear, every interval except the first being filled in with passing notes:

Ex.14

It will be noticed that the rising fourth at the start is followed by a stepwise descent as noted by Riezler in the Kyrie and other movements; also that the orchestra accompanies the subject with touches of imitation, given above in small notes. These additions are seldom audible in performance.

This fugue subject seems to have sprung from two quite different origins. The resemblance to Riezler's *leitmotiv* is not likely to have been conscious, but at any one period of time the same sort of ideas will be fermenting in a composer's mind, and those he chooses to incorporate in a work may show similarities which help to give that work unity even when the similarities are hard to detect. Both listener and composer may sense and welcome the unity without being fully aware of how it has been achieved.

But this applies only to the first five notes of the fugue subject. The basic sequence of rising fourths had been in Beethoven's mind for years. It may be remembered that the finale of the *Eroica* Symphony begins by paying attention to the bass of a tune that has not yet been heard:

Ex. 15

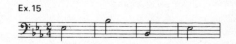

The Variations and Fugue for Piano, Op.35 which Beethoven wrote on this tune—it comes from his ballet, *The Creatures of Prometheus*—starts in a similar way, and in the final fugue of this work he develops the third and fourth notes of this bass as follows:

Ex.16

Nearly twenty years later Beethoven was writing another piano work, the Sonata in A flat, Op.110, and he ended it with a fugue whose subject is related (unconsciously?) to the very beginning of this sonata, and also to the fugue subject of the Gloria which Beethoven was writing at the same time:

Ex.17

The resemblance extends beyond the rising fourths to the stepwise descent in the last four notes. Beethoven finished the sonata on Christmas Day 1821 by which time he had already roughed out the fugue of the Gloria but he did not finalize it until later. It is hard to believe that he did not notice the resemblance, especially as both subjects were equally amenable to the fugal devices by which he was now obsessed. By this period he was bringing fugues into nearly all his works.

This interest in the fugue seems to have arisen from his having had access to a manuscript copy of Bach's '48' and to his possession of *The Art of Fugue*. After his death his pupil Carl Czerny published an edition of the '48' with editorial additions, and in the preface Czerny claimed that 'for the tempi and renderings' (Vortrag) he had been guided by 'the distinct remembrance I have of Beethoven's rendering of a great number of these fugues'.[3] This seems to imply that Beethoven played the fugues a great deal and the preludes hardly at all, which, with hindsight, is just what one would expect. It happens that the A major fugue in the First Book has a subject based on just such a series of rising fourths as the one in Beethoven's A flat Sonata.

I am not seriously suggesting that this fugue of Bach's influenced the one in the Gloria, but the '48' as a whole must surely have done so. They include examples of all the standard fugal devices—*stretto*, augmentation, diminution, inversion. But whereas Bach seldom used more than one of these devices in any one fugue, Beethoven liked to get in as many as possible. In the A flat Piano Sonata fugue he introduced inversion and augmentation (subject at half-speed) with splendid effect, and diminution (subject at double-speed) with some awkwardness for the pianist. In the Gloria fugue he again used augmentation magnificently, as also *stretto* and inversion. Both these fugues are triumphant successes.

For 67 bars the Gloria fugue is continuously *fortissimo*. To make it even louder than it was already Beethoven added trombones at the last moment; their parts do not occur in either the autograph or in the copy sent to the Archbishop. They double the altos, tenors and basses almost throughout, and though Beethoven left these trombone parts to his copyist he must have realized that unless care was taken the alto trombone might sometimes be faced with the impossible. On 28 September 1823 he was visited by a publisher, Tobias Haslinger, and an Englishman, Edward Schulz, who four months later described the meeting in the London *Harmonicon*.[4] 'He asked Haslinger about the highest possible note on the trombone but was dissatisfied with the answer which he received.' The question must have been prompted by the trombone parts being added in the Missa Solemnis, probably by those being added to the Gloria fugue. Perhaps as a result of Beethoven's advice the copyist left out the high Ds and Es in the alto trombone part (in bars 386–87 and 392–96 etc.) but a high D slipped by in bar 391. It cannot often have been played.*

Ex. 14 includes a counter-subject based on crotchets tied over the bar-line and first sung by the basses to the word 'Amen'. These tiny phrases are the foundation of those few passages in

---

*There is a very high trombone solo in Ravel's *Bolero* but the top note is D flat, a note found several times (as C sharp) in Beethoven's Gloria.

this opening peroration when the fugue subject itself is not being sung or played.

When the *fortissimo* ends the soloists, doubled only by the woodwind, have the subject in *stretto*:

Ex. 18

They then turn their attention to the counter-subject sung to 'Amen'. For several bars Beethoven has nothing on the first beats apart from notes tied over from the previous bar, and he modulates through so many keys in no time at all that chaos seems imminent; intrigued though we are, we are almost relieved when he lays anchor with a long-held pedal A and allows us to catch up with his thought processes. Above this A the chorus repeat the *stretto* and then the basses, followed by the altos and the sopranos, sing the subject in augmentation with the orchestra doubling them:

Ex. 19

It will be noticed that the tenors hint at the subject in its normal form. This is a superbly effective passage and the high B for the sopranos just before the end crowns the climax with an intense glory that is without parallel. To analyse a fugue is to risk making it sound dry. This one is in fact remarkably emotional.

Many composers would have ended the Gloria at this point, but Beethoven is bent on showing that he can cap even this climax. He starts the next section quietly with the soloists, but to guard against a slackening of tension he speeds up the tempo. Even so there is a danger that the audience's interest will briefly flag if only because what follows is so difficult to sing and we cannot but be aware of the difficulties. First the soloists have another run at the fugue subject, this time with a more flowing counter-subject and a minimum of orchestral accompaniment. Sections of the chorus support them unobtrusively, singing words from the 'Quoniam'. The tenor soloist then has the subject inverted:

Ex. 20

in   glo-ri-a De - i   pa - tris

but there is so much else going on that we are unlikely to notice. However, the soprano soloist also inverts the subject a bar or two later. These are the only occasions in the entire fugue when Beethoven resorts to this device and with one of them virtually inaudible his use of inversion can reasonably be described as half-hearted. He seems to have felt that without inversion no fugue was complete. He had flirted with the device in the Op.35 Variations for Piano and in the finale of the Third Rasumovsky Quartet, Op.59 no.3, and he used it with conviction in the Cello Sonata in D, Op.102 no.2, in the *Hammerklavier* Piano Sonata, Op.106, in the A flat Piano Sonata, Op.110, and in the fugue near the end of the *Diabelli* Variations, Op.120.

Within a bar or two of these inversions the whole chorus and most of the orchestra are thundering out the fugue subject in *fortissimo* unison, and with Beethoven emphasizing the chord of C major because he likes its modal implications when the key is D, and emphasizing too the word 'Amen' with its tied crotchets, the excitement becomes so extreme that we feel this really must be the end, no further climax being possible. But it is possible. Beethoven piles Pelion on Ossa with a Presto return to the opening of the Gloria. By now the excitement is verging on hysteria and the movement ends with a stroke of masterly dramatic invention—the chorus's final shouted 'gloria' is left hanging in mid-air, unaccompanied. Like the chorus, the audience now sits back with a sigh of sheer exhaustion, marvelling that any composer could have had so colossal and dramatic a vision of words which, in many churches, are all spoken quietly with no feeling of excitement whatsoever.

This is almost the first occasion on which a composer positively set out to overwhelm his audience. Martin Cooper has suggested that the very first time was in the fugue of the *Hammerklavier* Piano Sonata.

It is impossible, I think, to deny that there is in this finale, as in the Grosse Fuge, an element of excessiveness or what Coleridge called 'nimiety', an instinct to push every component part of the movement *à outrance*, not just to its logical conclusion but beyond. This instinct, which is more frequently found among German than any other artists and may well contain strongly aggressive elements, was to be indulged on an immense scale by Wagner.[5]

All this is equally applicable to the Gloria of the Missa Solemnis, as Cooper shows on a later page, and though 'nimiety' can also be detected in a number of works by Berlioz, notably the *Symphonie fantastique* which in its original form dates from a mere five or six years after the Missa Solemnis, it is certainly more a Germanic than a French characteristic and at its most extreme in the works of Wagner and Mahler and in the early works of Schoenberg.

I end this chapter with a warning for all those, myself included, who write too confidently about the influence of one composer upon another. The enormous fugue at the end of Beethoven's Gloria and the enormous fugue at the end of Mozart's Gloria in his Mass in C minor are outwardly so alike that influence seems certain. Mozart's fugue subject is also based on rising fourths though there is one less of them:

Ex. 21   Mozart

Furthermore he introduces both *stretto* and inversion, and even has his subject sung in *fortissimo* unison by the entire chorus. But Mozart never finished this Mass and it was not published until 1840; it is hardly possible that Beethoven ever set eyes on the music. I must add that as well as a resemblance there is also a great difference between these two fugues. Mozart's, it seems to me, is clever, uncharacteristic and rather arid; Beethoven's is less clever, strongly characteristic and excitingly emotional from start to finish.

6
Credo

In two senses the Credo is central to any setting of the Mass, and it will almost certainly be the longest movement, there being more words to set than there are in all the other movements put together. These words present the composer with problems he does not need to face elsewhere, and the chief problem is that in the Credo there are events; something happens, if only in the middle section. Christ came down from Heaven and was born of the Virgin Mary; after being crucified and buried he rose again and ascended into Heaven. There are six events here, and each can be depicted in music of descriptive intent. Indeed, no baroque or classical composer known to me has been able to resist treating at least some of them with musical symbolism. But working against the composer's natural urge for the dramatic must be the solemnity of the Credo as a whole. Many will feel that this blueprint for the Christian faith should not be subjected to the vulgarity (if that is the word) of dramatic treatment, however much this is underplayed. The words must also raise in the composer's mind questions about what he himself believes in, for this is likely to colour the way he sets them. Like many other people he may well find some parts of the Credo more convincing than others, and it has been suggested that Beethoven hurried through certain phrases towards the end precisely because he had doubts about them.

As in the Gloria the music divides roughly into three sections, fast—slow—fast, and these sections will be discussed separately.

Credo in unum Deum, Patrem omnipotentem, factorem coeli et terrae, visibilium omnium et invisibilium; et in unum Dominum Jesum Christum, filium Dei uni-

I believe in one God the Father Almighty, maker of heaven and earth, and of all things visible and invisible; and in one Lord Jesus Christ, the only-begotten Son of

genitum, et ex patre natum ante omnia saecula, Deum de Deo, lumen de lumine, Deum verum de Deo vero, genitum, non factum, consubstantialem Patris per quem omnia facta sunt; qui propter nos homines et propter nostram salutem descendit de coelis,

God, begotten of his Father before all worlds, God of God, Light of Light, very God of very God, begotten, not made, being of one substance with the Father, by whom all things were made: who for us men and for our salvation came down from heaven,

No one need be surprised that Beethoven's sketches for the start of the Credo verge on the inept; his preliminary sketches often do. He seems to have needed to write down something which (to us) looks totally unpromising before he could find what he wanted:

Later he found a better rhythm for this:

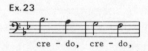

but the phrase still lacks conviction. Perhaps his thoughts then turned to the fragment of plainsong that is traditionally intoned by the priest at the start of the movement.* In this the word 'Credo' suggests a serene certainty quite lacking in Beethoven's sketches because it is sung to the falling third that reflects the way the word is commonly said. Accordingly he devised a four-note theme (see Ex.25) which features this falling third, and he was surely aware that this added to the unity of the Mass as a whole.

But Beethoven did not begin with this theme. He was so careful to relate his opening bars to the end of the Gloria that ideally there should be as little gap between the movements as possible. B flat is his chosen key as it is for the slow movement of the Ninth Symphony (also in D) and as it so often is for

*Bach, unknown to Beethoven, had used this very phrase as a fugue subject at the start of the Credo in his B minor Mass.

contrasting sections in both works. But Beethoven does not start his Credo in this key. Instead, he surprises us with a chord of E flat, a mere semitone above the final chord of the Gloria. But this does not sound quite as strange as you would expect. Here are the final bars of the Gloria followed by the opening bars of the Credo:

Ex. 24

The pivotal note is G. Because it has occurred several times at the top of the harmony in the closing bars of the Gloria, it sounds reasonable enough at the top of the first chord in the Credo, and our surprise is limited to the unexpected way it is harmonized. The transition is masterly. And even more striking in 1824 when people expected the Credo to be in the same key as the Gloria. Beethoven has changed key one movement earlier than usual.

After these four bars for the orchestra, the chorus initiates what is virtually a double fugue on two very short subjects, of which the top one is to prove much the more important:

Ex. 25

Any teacher of counterpoint would blue-pencil the lower subject for it results in a succession of consecutive octaves, yet I doubt if anyone has ever been worried by this in performance. What strikes one is the fervour of the music. This results mainly from the choice of notes for the word Credo, but partly as well from the *sforzandi* and from the trombones who double many of the entries. Indeed they double the chorus for most of this opening Allegro section though not mechanically as in the Gloria fugue. Animated semiquavers for the violins add to the effect.

It will be remembered that at the first performance of the Credo in 1824 the sopranos of the chorus complained bitterly about what they were expected to sing. Some 20 bars into the Credo they are faced by the following enormity:

Ex. 26

In modern full-length performances the sopranos will already have fought their way through a similar passage in the final Presto of the Gloria where, in 11 consecutive bars without rests, their *lowest* note is high G. When Beethoven refused to alter such passages he may have been recalling the high B flats that Haydn gave his sopranos in his *Nelson* Mass; most unusually for him, Haydn even asks for a high B natural early on in the Gloria and another in the final fugue which, being preceded by an octave leap, is so difficult as to be virtually unsingable. But these are isolated notes; what makes Beethoven's writing for the sopranos so much more difficult is that he keeps them above the stave for bar after bar, which Haydn never did.

Beethoven plans to return to his main Credo theme towards the end of the movement, and in order to establish it the more firmly in the listener's mind he repeats his more-or-less fugal exposition, indulging in some imaginative dynamic extremes—*pp* for 'ante omnia saecula' and *ff* for 'Deum de Deo'—and giving the words 'Deum' and 'Deo' falling thirds like those which by now we are associating with the word 'Credo'. Perhaps he had a subtle doctrinal purpose. Because his themes have so far been very short he now guards against fragmentation with a long stolid and almost Handelian theme treated fugally. It is unlikely that Beethoven was conscious of its faint similarity to the crotchet theme in Ex.5:

Ex. 27

The bass entry is cut short but the soprano one contributes to a
miniscule *stretto*, the tenors singing much the same notes one bar
later.

The woodwind, of which we have not so far been conscious,
become audible from bar 87 onwards, and I give the bar number
to indicate the degree of their previous eclipse. We can hear them
now because Beethoven chooses quiet music for 'Qui propter nos
homines et propter nostram salutem', but he does not delay on
these words, being in a hurry to reach the all-important 'descendit
de coelis'. From the first he treats these words symbolically:

Ex. 28

Because Heaven was conventionally thought of as being high in
the sky, Beethoven always sets 'coelis' to high notes—in the above
example to notes that even today will be too high for many
basses. In case we miss his symbolism he makes it even more
explicit in the extraordinary choral outburst that ends this
opening section of the Credo:

Ex.29

Et incarnatus est de Spiritu Sancto ex Maria Virgine, et homo factus est; Crucifixus etiam pro nobis; sub Pontio Pilato passus et sepultus est;

And was incarnate by the Holy Ghost of the Virgin Mary, and was made man, and was crucified also for us under Pontius Pilate. He suffered and was buried;

Beethoven set these words to music of great intensity, full of descriptive touches of various kinds. For the first nine words he combined the unusual simplicity of two-part counterpoint with modalism, and the result is mysterious and awesome:

Ex.30

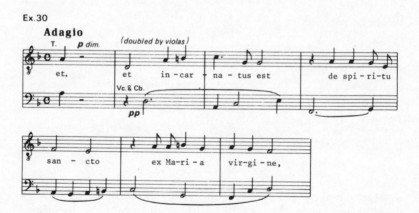

Violas double the voice. Beethoven's inspired use of the Lydian Mode stemmed from advice he received about the mediaeval modes and their implications from a friend who worked as librarian to Prince Lobkowitz. The autograph score has these words sung by the chorus tenors, but in the first published edition

they are given to the tenor soloist. Willy Hess, editor of the
Eulenburg miniature score, accepts this as evidence that Beethov-
en changed his mind, but most editions follow the autograph and
the early copies, as do virtually all modern conductors.

All four soloists develop this theme with gentle reverence, and
Beethoven was careful to mark down the string accompaniment
so that they could do so quietly. The voices are doubled by 'a
few' violins and specifically by two violas and two cellos while
a flute offers unexpected but unmistakable birdsong. 'There is
no reasonable doubt,' wrote Tovey, 'that the picture in Beethoven's mind is that of the Holy Ghost hovering in the likeness
of a dove.'[1] But there is reasonable doubt in that the bird does
not sound in the least like a dove. As a symbol of the Holy Ghost
the dove derives from the account in St Mark's Gospel i:10 of
Jesus being baptized in the Jordan. 'And straightway coming up
out of the water he saw the heavens opened and the Spirit like
a dove descending upon him.' Religious encyclopaedias and
dictionaries usually mention the dove as a symbol in connection
with Our Lord's baptism but not, so far as I can discover, with
His Annunciation and Birth. A dove is shown fluttering above
the Angel and Mary in some Renaissance paintings of the
Annunciation but not in all; for instance, in at least two by
Tintoretto in the San Rocco in Venice but not in the more famous
one by Fra Angelico in Florence. We shall never know what
paintings of this subject Beethoven knew, but he surely did know
Haydn's *Schöpfungmesse*. In this the 'Incarnatus est' is accompanied by an organ solo marked Flauto in the autograph and
Flautino (piccolo; i.e. a 4 foot stop) in the first edition.[2] Haydn
had to use the organ because at the time there were no flutes in
the orchestra. But whereas Haydn's organ part is no more than
a vague suggestion of birdsong, Beethoven's flute part sounds like
direct imitation. The trouble is that the trills and chirpings are
much more like a blackbird, thrush or robin; either Beethoven
had forgotten what a dove sounded like or he was aiming at a
generalized pastoral scene rather than religious symbolism.

When these same words are intoned on one note, *pianissimo*,
by the whole chorus, the effect is for a brief moment like the
murmured undertones of the congregation at a normal church
service. After a dozen radiant bars for the incarnation we come
to the slowest and most solemn music in the whole work:

Ex. 31

The off-beat *sforzandi* are surely meant to suggest nails being hammered into the body on the cross, and the heavy octaves that follow for 'sub Pontio Pilato' to suggest the ruthless power of the Roman overlords. Beethoven dwells with horror on 'passus'; the false relation for the orchestra, C natural against C sharp, precisely reflects Christ's suffering, and the first violin phrases sound the more mournful for being doubled an octave below by a bassoon:

Ex. 32

This comes again later but it is never sung. Voices and strings subside semitone by semitone at the words 'et sepultus est'—more symbolism here—and this intensely-felt slow section seems to be about to end *ppp*. Before it can quite do so there is a marvellous radiant interruption.

Et resurrexit tertia die secundum Scripturas; et ascendit in coelum; sedet ad dexteram Patris, et iterum venturus est cum gloria judicare vivos et mortuos, cujus regni non erit finis; (Credo) et in Spiritum Sanctum Dominum et vivificantem, qui ex patre filioque procedit, qui cum patre et filio simul adoratur et conglorificatur, qui locutus est per Prophetas, et in unam sanctam catholicam et apostolicam ecclesiam, confiteor unum baptisma in remissionem peccatorum, et exspecto resurrectionem mortuorum, et vitam venturi saeculi. Amen.

And the third day he rose again according to the scriptures, and ascended into heaven, and sitteth on the right hand of the Father. And he shall come again with glory to judge both the quick and the dead: whose kingdom shall have no end. And I believe in the Holy Ghost, the Lord, the Giver of life, who proceedeth from the Father and the Son, who with the Father and the Son together is worshipped and glorified, who spake by the prophets. And I believe in one holy catholic and apostolic Church. I acknowledge one Baptism for the remission of sins. And I look for the Resurrection of the dead, and the Life of the world to come. Amen.

Ex.33

This six-bar outburst is extraordinarily dramatic. Quite apart from the sudden loudness we are unprepared both for its being unaccompanied and for its being modal. Tovey describes the mode as 'Mixolydian as Palestrina would conceive it' and calls this 'the only unaccompanied choral passage in any Mass of the period'. This is not strictly accurate but the remark does convey the essential truth that these bars are unlike any others in classical music.

This is as good a time as any to consider just how far Beethoven's modal writing derives from Palestrina. Not much of his music was then in print and what there was had usually been rebarred by editors who thought that every bar should have four beats. This happened to the famous *Stabat Mater* for double choir which Palestrina had written in the homophonic style because the Council of Trent had recently asked composers to avoid counterpoint in the interests of verbal clarity. Beethoven almost certainly knew this work; Palestrina's homophonic style seems to have appealed to him more than this composer's contrapuntal writing. Half way through the *Stabat Mater* Palestrina's chords bear a faint resemblance to Beethoven's though this passage is not noticeably modal. For the sake of simplicity and to save space I give only the gist of the music, which, at least at the start, is in eight parts:

Ex.34

Perhaps Beethoven had this passage in mind but it is much more likely that he was influenced by Palestrina in only the most general way. It is astonishingly easy to find Palestrina influence where in fact there can be none at all. Some 50 bars from the end of the Gloria in Beethoven's Mass in C there is a Palestrina-like progression of chords, yet no one has ever suggested that in 1807 Beethoven felt much interest in or had any real knowledge of modal music.

As in so many Masses, Christ ascends to Heaven to the sound of quick symbolically rising scales, and Beethoven saw the remaining words in this paragraph as an opportunity for exhilaration, the only such opportunity in the Credo. For most of this section the words are set to such simple chords that the voices seem to be accompanying the orchestra, and the violins have the only memorable tune:

Ex. 35

After he had finished the autograph Beethoven came to feel that this little phrase needed a little more space if it were to register and he added a couple of bars here and two more in a similar passage a little later at the point where the tenors repeat the word 'et'. The bustling stops for four bars so that Beethoven can treat 'judicare' with proper solemnity, and here too he had second thoughts; the accompanying trombone parts had originally been given to the horns. He now found himself in the key of G flat with C flats all over the place, and his sketch books show that he tried to reduce the awkwardness by going into F sharp major, but this only made things worse still so he restored the flats. At 'vivos' he at one time had A double flats for the entire orchestra and chorus but he managed to struggle out of this predicament. It is typical of his thinking while composing the Missa Solemnis that 'vivos' is sung to *fortissimo* detached crotchets with full accompaniment whereas immediately afterwards 'mortuos' is sung to long-held *piano* notes with scarcely any accompaniment at all. He seized on every opportunity for extreme dramatic contrasts.

The little violin phrase quoted above returns immediately after this contrast, and the chorus sings a profusion of falling thirds to the words 'cujus regni non erit finis'. Astonishingly, Beethoven ends this paragraph by abstracting the word 'non' and having the chorus almost shout it three times to detached crotchets in bare octaves. 'Does it not seem', wrote Willy Hess in the Eulenburg score, 'that he is battling within himself for his belief in immortality?'

The second and longer paragraph in this final quick section of the Credo returns to the details of Christian belief and accordingly Beethoven brings back his opening theme on the trombones and other wind instruments. What follows virtually amounts to a development section. He is much more interested in his Credo theme than in the words he now has to set, so much so that 'Credo' is sung in every one of the next 19 bars and with *sforzandi* abounding and trombones doubling we have very little chance of hearing what the other words are. Even if he had omitted all these dominating 'Credos' we would miss many of the words for Beethoven has the phrases overlapping as sometimes in a Mozart Missa Brevis. He actually gets from 'Credo in spiritum sanctum' to 'per Prophetas' in 11 bars and though this is not a record—in a setting already mentioned for its extreme brevity, the *Organ Solo* Mass, K.259, Mozart managed these words in nine—it is a more extreme example of compression than one can readily find in any other Mass, and the more extraordinary for occurring in this one when brevity was no object.

There are three possible explanations, and Beethoven may have been motivated by more than one of them. He may have felt little interest or even belief in the Holy Ghost and for that reason made all references inaudible on purpose. He may have become aware that he had already written at great length in the first part of the Credo and planned to write at great length in the final fugue, and he therefore thought he should save as much time as possible over the words he thought mattered least. He may have been trying to suggest a crowd inspired by an almost pentecostal ecstasy with a profusion of 'Credos' flung at the audience from all sections of the chorus:

Ex. 36

The last is the most attractive explanation. The passage is certainly effective and quite different from the corresponding one in the Mass in C; there the words that take 11 bars in the Missa Solemnis take 25. Haydn and many other composers had almost always had 'credo in unam sanctam catholicam et apostolicam ecclesiam' sung by the chorus in octave unison to symbolize the church's unity, and Beethoven had followed this age-old convention in his Mass in C. But in the Missa Solemnis these words are sung only by the tenors and rendered inaudible by the 'Credos' for the sopranos and altos.

It is unlikely but possible that Beethoven had seen manuscript scores of some of Mozart's early Masses. He could have found models of a sort for his 'Credo' repetitions in both the Mass in F, K.192 and the *Credo* Mass, K.257 though Mozart does not let this word overlap the others. When Vincent Novello edited the *Credo* Mass in the 1840s he was so shocked by the unliturgical repetition of 'Credo' that he cut all these bars out. One would expect strict Catholics to be at least as shocked by this passage in the Missa Solemnis but I have come on no evidence that they were.

Beethoven ended his Credo with a fugue that was as long as the one in the Gloria and even more difficult to sing. It was indeed the most difficult music that any chorus had ever had to face apart from the end of the Ninth Symphony which Beethoven wrote at much the same time. In August 1819 Schindler visited Beethoven at his lodgings in Mödling just outside Vienna.

It was four o'clock in the afternoon. As soon as we entered we were told that both Beethoven's maids had left that morning and that there had occurred after midnight an uproar that had disturbed everyone in the house because, having waited so long, both maids had gone to sleep and the meal they had prepared was inedible. From behind the closed door of one of the parlours we could hear the master working on the fugue of the Credo, singing, yelling, stamping his feet. When we had heard enough of this almost frightening performance and were about to depart, the door opened and Beethoven stood before us, his features distorted to the point of inspiring terror. He looked as though he had just engaged in a life and death struggle with the whole army of contrapuntists, his everlasting enemies. His first words were confused, as if he felt embarrassed at having been overheard. Soon he began to speak of the day's events and said, with noticeable self-control, 'What a mess! Everyone has run away and I haven't had anything to eat since yesterday noon'. . . Never has such a great work of art been created under such adverse living conditions as this Missa Solemnis. . .[3]

This account coupled with the fugue's extreme difficulty may have contributed to the view often held by conductors in the past that it was a colossus. In short, it has often been performed too loudly and too fast. Beethoven was well aware that he had already written a fugal colossus at the end of the Gloria and that he now needed something quite different in mood and effect. The Credo fugue has a less energetic tempo, a marvellously unconventional main subject, and a strictly rationed number of climaxes. The Allegretto marking implies more than a tempo slower than Allegro; it also asks for an almost dance-like delicacy and this, though hard to achieve, is essential for success. The fugue resembles the one in the Gloria only in its profusion of devices. Inversion and diminution are admirably used and touches of *stretto* can also be found, but the main subject is too slow for augmentation just as the main subject in the Gloria fugue is too fast for diminution.

This is a double fugue; the subject in minims proves more fruitful than the one in crotchets:

Ex.37

Allegretto ma non troppo

(doubled by woodwind and lower strings)

There is a resemblance here, presumably unconscious, to the 'Christe' themes in the middle of the Kyrie. There too the time signature was three-two, and not only did the main theme in minims feature descending thirds but the subsidiary theme for the most part moved stepwise in crotchets. But the gentle dancing mood of the Credo fugue cannot be paralleled in the Kyrie. It is emphasized by the staccato dots that Beethoven put on nearly all the minims in the orchestral parts, and there is much to be said for the chorus singing their minims with equal lightness and, as conductors sometimes put it, with daylight between the notes. Beethoven adds to the delicacy of the accompaniment by silencing his violins throughout the opening section (some 60 bars long) and by letting flutes, clarinets and bassoons do most of the doubling. The harsher-sounding oboes are used only sparingly.

The trouble is that it is impossible to sing some of this fugue with what I have called dance-like delicacy:

Ex. 38

Stupefied by these outrageous demands on the sopranos we may
not notice that the alto entry is never completed and that this is
not a true *stretto*, but Beethoven manages much more cleverly
when he starts inverting his two subjects—the basses are the first
to invert the one in minims—and he brings off a technical *tour
de force* when he contrives to have both subjects both ways up
at the same time:

Ex. 39

(For the sake of clarity I have omitted the less essential parts.)
Fragments of the two subjects then rise in sequence with fine
effect to a climax in which Beethoven again comes near to
achieving a *stretto* but does not disappoint in not quite managing
it.

The tempo quickens, dynamics drop to *pianissimo*, and the
violins break their long silence to play fragments of the minim
theme in diminution against its original form in the bass:

The woodwind phrases herald a new counter-subject, and the
tied quavers that give it individuality also make it desperately
difficult to sing:

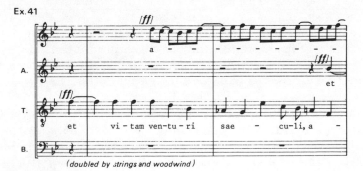

(*doubled by strings and woodwind*)

Nowhere in the Missa Solemnis does Beethoven make such unreasonable demands on his chorus as here; by no stretch of the imagination can the next 20 bars be said to offer good vocal writing. The passage hardly ever quite comes off.

It may be noticed that diminution has shifted the accents in the main fugue subject; also that at the end of the passage quoted above a third subject has been introduced consisting of rising sixths (or fifths) sung to the word 'Amen'. As in the Gloria fugue, difficulties melt away as soon as Beethoven anchors his music to a dominant pedal, in this case an F, and he now builds up a superb climax mainly remarkable for its extraordinary emotional effect. We may also notice that in the course of it he manages to have his minim subject sung in octaves by the chorus at the same time as the strings and bass trombone are playing it in diminution.

We expect the fugue to end within a matter of seconds, and when it doesn't we wonder if Beethoven is planning to work up to a yet more astonishing climax as at the end of the Gloria fugue. Wisely he does nothing of the kind. He brings back his soloists who have not been heard since the slow middle section of the Credo and, as Tovey puts it, the 'grand cadence dies away with Beethoven's favourite choral effect of suddenly receding into the depths of the universe. And then the heavens open.' But not with overwhelming grandeur; rather with overwhelming peace. The effect is achieved with the simplest symbolism. Each soloist in turn sings 'Amen' to quavers that seem to float up to the top of the compass; most of the strings and a solo flute float up too, as indeed, after the interruption of two *fortissimo* choral 'Amens' (from down on earth?) do all the woodwind. Against the ascending woodwind scales in thirds and sixths the strings play very simple, slow, gentle, falling scales as though grace descends from Heaven as our prayers rise up.

The magnificent and seemingly endless series of crossing scales at the end of the Credo, which seem to go ever higher and lower like a Jacob's ladder as the complexity of sound hides the new beginnings, must be accepted as Beethoven's audible image of eternity, and they are the equivalent of the words, 'I believe in the life to come, world without end, Amen'.[4]

The life to come. This thought is indeed paramount in Beethoven's mind for in the very last bars, when the singers and most of the orchestra are very quietly holding a final chord of B flat, the trombones and the bass strings playing *pizzicato* delicately touch in the first half-dozen notes of the minim fugue subject, the very notes to which 'et vitam venturi' was sung at the start. The reference is so subtle that not all conductors seem aware of it.

If there is to be an interval of two or three minutes, this is where it should come.

7

Sanctus and Benedictus

Sanctus, sanctus, sanctus, Dominus Deus Sabaoth. Pleni sunt coeli et terra gloria tua. Osanna in excelsis.

Holy, holy, holy, Lord God of Hosts. Heaven and earth are full of thy glory. Hosanna in the highest.

Benedictus qui venit in nomine Domini. Osanna in excelsis.

Blessed is he who cometh in the name of the Lord. Hosanna in the highest.

In both his Masses Beethoven followed Haydn's usual practice and set the first of the paragraphs shown above in three short contrasted sections and the second paragraph in one long section. In the Missa Solemnis the Benedictus is even longer than usual. Beethoven wrote it in a key he had scarcely touched on earlier, G major, but he had restored D major for the three short Sanctus sections because, with his Credo in B flat and his Agnus Dei in B minor, he did not want to lose sight of his main key for too long. After all, in his four-movement symphonies there is never more than one movement in an alien key.

It is in fact some bars before we are aware of what key he has chosen for the Sanctus. This is yet another transition he planned with very great care. Bassoons and double basses begin softly in what appears to be B minor; the very first note is a low B. This is a semitone above the B flats that dominate the last chord of the Credo, just as the E flats at the start of that movement are a semitone above the Ds at the end of the Gloria. These are surprising juxtapositions. In the *Hammerklavier* Sonata Beethoven had surprised with similar juxtapositions but in the other direction; the Scherzo ends in B flat and the slow movement starts with octave As, and then the slow movement ends in F sharp and the subsequent Largo begins with octave Fs. In both works we feel something quite new is in gestation. Haydn had sometimes begun a Sanctus loudly; Beethoven not only starts softly but keeps his dynamics at a low level. He uses solo voices without the chorus, cuts out violins, flutes and oboes, and has his brass instruments playing quietly for almost the first time in the work. The mood is a combination of humility and awe.

Deaf though he was, Beethoven had not forgotten the subtle difference between the sound of a horn, a trumpet and a trombone and he is soon contrasting the three tone colours in a tight-packed way that had not, so far as I am aware, been tried before. (I give the actual sounds, not the notes as printed.)

Ex.42

The horns are doubled by lower woodwind and strings, the trumpets by the timpani. When the solo voices come in, they are accompanied by the phrases on bassoons and lower strings, starting with the low B, which we heard at the very start of the movement:

Ex.43

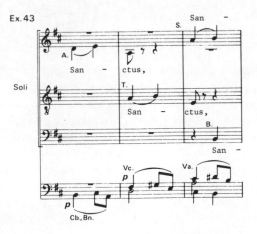

The violas and cellos are already *divisi*, that is, playing in close four-part harmony. In the absence of the brighter-sounding treble instruments the music has a sombre hue. The Sanctus ends with a soft drum roll above which the violas and cellos play a shimmering dominant ninth that sinks to a *pianissimo*. Such an ending arouses expectation; in Beethoven it is almost bound to be suddenly interrupted by a great blaze of sound from the whole orchestra. This indeed is what happens.

'Pleni sunt coeli' is set as a sort of joyous fugue only 19 bars long and loud throughout. The sound is very bright, with the violins returning to play extravert semiquavers and the first flute holding from the start a top A which was at the time of composition its highest and most piercing note. The music is not a strict fugue for each entry starts a third below the one before:

Ex.44

As in previous movements Beethoven cannot resist symbolism. Once he had decided that 'coeli' must have high notes and 'terra' low ones, the fugue subject almost wrote itself. In its context this tiny movement sounds wonderfully vigorous and fresh.

There is a problem about the voice parts. With the entire orchestra playing loudly in every bar you would think it went without saying that they were intended for the chorus, but the autograph and the first printed score both appear to ask that the soloists heard in the Sanctus should continue to sing in both the 'Pleni sunt coeli' and in the equally loud 'Osanna'. This would mean that from the start of the Sanctus the chorus would not sing at all for about a quarter of an hour. In 1857 a performance of the Missa Solemnis was given in Bonn during a congress of scientists and physicians, and both these loud sections were sung by the soloists. One of the critics pointed out that they could scarcely be heard and he wondered if the vocal parts were really meant for the chorus. Schindler, by now an old gentleman making all he could out of his friendship with Beethoven, was asked his opinion, and he claimed that when he was helping Beethoven correct the manuscript copies of the Missa Solemnis that were to be sent to the crowned heads of Europe, 'I remarked that it seemed to me the two movements would be more effective if sung by full chorus than if sung by four solo voices... Beethoven replied at length, but the substance was that "Solo voices it must be".'[1] As Schindler realized, the balance between singers and orchestra was made even worse by Beethoven tempo, Allegro pesante, for heaviness would be the last quality required if so large an orchestra were accompanying single voices. Nevertheless, disregarding what, according to him, were Beethoven wishes, Schindler advocated the use of a chorus.

It seems to me inconceivable that Beethoven would have written such an accompaniment for four soloists and marked it 'pesante'. On the other hand it would be a very natural mistake to write chorus parts on the same staves he had used in the Sanctus for the soloists and forget to indicate the change. It was not unknown for Schindler to make something up when he could not remember what had happened, and in any case he would not want it revealed that he himself had missed this mistake when going through the score with the composer. A conscientious modern editor has little alternative but to print the parts as for soloists, adding an editorial comment, and that is what Willy Hess has done in the Eulenburg score, but most vocal scores, including Novello's, mark both sections as for 'Coro' and that is how they are nearly always sung. Only Otto Klemperer, I think, has recorded these two sections for soloists, and he did so in both his 1953 and his 1966 recordings, but though it may be just possible to balance solo voices against the orchestra in a recording studio it is not possible in concert conditions.

The 'Osanna' is a more conventional fugue than the 'Pleni sunt coeli':

Ex.45

Sforzandi are scattered wholesale on the orchestral staves, often three to a bar. The Presto marking results in a playing time of only half a minute. The final chord is unexpected and effective.

This is where the break comes in all other Masses to allow for the Elevation of the Host, and the Benedictus can be expected to follow after a gap of a minute or less. Beethoven fills this gap with a Praeludium for orchestra intended as a background to the Elevation. This would seem to conflict with the rubric of the Roman Missal which lays down that the choir must be silent at this point, though it is not clear whether an orchestra, if present, must be silent too. Beethoven's innovation has been much commented on. I doubt if the writing of this Praeludium was his own idea. It may well have been suggested to him by the Archduke. Austrian organists sometimes extemporized quietly to fill up the gap and the Archduke would certainly have preferred something by Beethoven to an organist's doodle. Olmütz was after all to be his own cathedral.

Beethoven was probably trying to suggest both organ tone and extemporization. He scored the Praeludium for *divisi* violas and cellos, with flutes more or less doubling the violas until the notes get too low for them when clarinets take over. A bassoon and double basses support the bass line. The music is low-lying and rather dense in texture; perhaps Viennese organists tended to keep their extemporizations to the lower half of the keyboard. It is also quietly meditative and not obviously tuneful. Beethoven seems to have gone out of his way not to distract the audience-congregation from 'adoring' the Host, as the Missal puts it.

Over the final chord we suddenly hear a solo violin and two flutes high in their compass, and the Benedictus has begun. The three close-knit strands slowly descend, symbolizing the Real Presence of Christ coming down from heaven to earth and entering the Host. The chorus basses softly intone the six words of the Benedictus. There is no other religious work, wrote Tovey, 'in which the idea of accomplishing a miracle, the descent of something divine, has been more simply and convincingly expressed.' The solo violin has concerto status; for a good ten minutes the player dominates the music as though engaged on a concerto slow movement. The mood is serene and relaxed, which means that it is unlike any other section of the work. Arguably the mood is a little too relaxed, yet the writing for solo violin is celestially lovely. Its first tune has an unusual accompaniment, and a second follows almost at once:

Ex.46 a)

(lower wind and pizzicato cellos)

The *pianissimo* chords for brass show that Beethoven knew more about trombone potentialities than we might have expected from a study of the earlier movements. According to Tovey, when Sir Michael Costa conducted the Benedictus in the middle of the nineteenth century he decided that these trombone chords were a cheap dance music cliché, and to Tovey's fully-justified indignation he crossed them out.[2] In fact they are not only musically pleasing but also subtly allusive, for the instruments seem to be quietly murmuring the word 'Benedictus'. They are still doing so when the soloists are first heard, singing the violin's opening tune in canon at the unusual interval of a seventh:

Beethoven contrapuntal ingenuities often show signs of struggle; this one is so effortless and felicitous that we may not notice it. Such canons, wrote Tovey, 'have a special accent of pleading, because the second voice repeats the phrases of the first a step higher in the scale', and he cites similar instances in the Recordare from Mozart's Requiem and in one of the variations in the central movement of Beethoven's String Quartet in C sharp minor.

The other two soloists repeat the canon higher up as befits their different vocal range and the texture thickens a little. A new theme for the solo violin is imitated by the clarinet, an instrument that is to be given increasing prominence as the movement proceeds:

Ex.48

By now the chorus are contributing to the gentle sounds, accompanying the solo violin rather than singing any actual tunes of their own. Beethoven moves into C major for a dozen bars so that the solo violin may play Ex.46 in a higher and therefore more celestial key. Brass and timpani are still murmuring the Benedictus rhythm in the background. All the tunes come round again either on the solo violin or sung by the solo singers, and eventually it is time for Beethoven to consider the final 'Osanna in excelsis'. As we have seen, he cannot repeat the ecstatic 'Osanna' heard just before the Praeludium if only because it was in the wrong key. The new 'Osanna' is suitably restrained, though Beethoven does raise the dynamic level to *forte* and give his under-employed chorus a new fugato:

Ex.49

But is this fugue subject new? Consciously or not, Beethoven has returned to that germinal motive he has used so often already—a leap of a fourth followed by a stepwise descent to the starting-point (and in this case beyond it). There are no more than nine bars of this and they end on a climax and a pause. What will come next, we wonder. Very gently the solo violin returns to Ex.46b, and the chorus, not so gently, to their fugue subject in close canon, and the movements ends.

Some listeners find the Benedictus a little too long. This is partly because Beethoven has been so excitingly concise in the Sanctus, Pleni sunt coeli and Osanna; we are not conditioned to meditate at length during what comes next, and need a conscious effort of will to acclimatize our minds to the slower time-scale and reduced demands on our concentration. The effort of will is, needless to add, worth making. If we drowse into a semi-coma we will miss such unassertive felicities as the quiet singing by the chorus in simple octaves. This happens twice and the emotional effect is out of all proportion to the means used which seem almost naive. Beethoven may have got the device from the *Nelson* Mass in which Haydn has his chorus in octaves much more frequently than in any of his other Masses, and perhaps most memorably in the 'Qui tollis' of the Gloria. Beethoven's serenely lyrical and gentle Benedictus is an admirable foil to the intense and deeply-felt Agnus Dei which comes next.

Among those who thought the Benedictus would have been even better if it had been shorter was Busoni. In 1915 he published an arrangement of it for solo violin and orchestra. He kept the Praeludium, scarcely changed the solo violin part, gave the music for the solo voices so far as possible to an oboe, a solo viola and a solo cello, and cut from eight bars after the return to G major to the eleventh bar from the end—bars 187 to 223 as numbered in the Eulenburg score. Violinists either do not know of this arrangement's existence or feel they would lose caste if they played it.

8
Agnus Dei

Agnus Dei, qui tollis peccata mundi,	O Lamb of God, who takest away the sins of the world,
miserere nobis.	have mercy upon us.
Agnus Dei, qui tollis peccata mundi,	O Lamb of God, who takest away the sins of the world,
dona nobis pacem.	give us peace.

From these two short sentences Beethoven contrives a movement of considerable complexity, as long as either the Gloria or Sanctus, which means that it plays for more than a quarter of an hour. Like most composers he makes a separate movement out of the last three words (though there is no break) and it is at this point that he returns to his starting key, D major. But not all the Dona was to be in this key. For reasons we shall come to later, Beethoven had already planned a contrasting section in B flat, the key to which he keeps turning in the Missa Solemnis, and from the first he has his trumpets crooked in this key and his timpani tuned to B flat and low F because he needs to feature them in his contrasting section. But the Agnus Dei starts in B minor in which key his trumpets can play only one note and his timpani none at all; he manages very well without them. Beethoven hardly ever wrote in B minor, a key he is said to have found oppressively dark.

For more than half the Agnus Dei he emphasizes B minor darkness, concentrating on the lower voices and lower instruments, and giving prominence to the melancholy qualities of the bassoon:

Ex. 50

The falling third at the start of this theme links the Agnus Dei to the earlier movements and foreshadows the way Beethoven sets the word 'miserere' a few bars later. The chord at bar 3 contributes to the pessimistic mood of the music. Against the 'misereres' the orchestra has:

Ex. 51

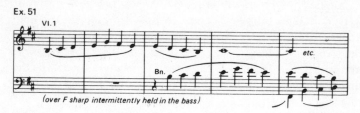

Ex. 50 returns with the clarinet playing the bassoon's theme and the alto and tenor soloists sharing the vocal line. When all this comes round for the third time the dynamic is *fortissimo*; the human tragedy is lamented by all four soloists and we scarcely notice the chorus joining in with *pianissimo* repetitions of 'miserere nobis' or the first violins playing continuous non-thematic quavers for more than 20 bars against the crotchets and minims of the singers. This violin part suggests a background of mourning, perhaps even of wailing, and it is enough if we pick up the sound intermittently. There is a parallel passage in the slow movement of Elgar's Second Symphony at the point where the tune heard near the start returns like a funeral march while an oboe, wailing as it were in the distance, plays continuous triplet quavers of which we are only occasionally aware.

The gloom of this section is total. Nowhere does Beethoven seem to sense that underlying comfort which other composers have found in the words. After all, if Christ takes away the sins of the world there must be hope for all of us. Beethoven feels little or no hope that his sins will be forgiven, but he believes passionately that Christ can and will bring peace to the world. Thus at the double-bar which separates the two sections of this movement pessimism gives way to a rather dubious optimism. It is highly significant that at this point in the score Beethoven wrote 'Bitte um innern und äussern Frieden', which means 'Prayer for both inner and outer peace'. Outer peace was for the world, and it had come with the ending of the Napoleonic Wars in 1815. Inner peace was what Beethoven himself so desperately needed and could not find. The frustration of his deafness, his increasing stomach pains, and the behaviour of his nephew, Karl, combined to make his inner life a continual catastrophe, and he prayed for relief in the first half of the Agnus Dei. The Dona shows that Beethoven had more hope for terrestrial peace than for personal forgiveness.

His note-books show that at first he searched for a 'peace' tune of total simplicity on the lines of the 'joy' theme which, it so happened, he was searching for at the same time; a tune in D major which moved stepwise within a small compass and in a simple rhythm:

Ex. 52

Assai sostenuto

Do - na,   do - na   no - bis pa - cem

Later he decided to distinguish between 'dona' and 'pacem'. The former required a falling interval to suggest an imploring tone of voice and he eventually chose that same falling third he had so often used for important words in the Missa Solemnis. He provided yet more links with previous movements by tying notes across the barlines and thereby eliminating main beats so that accents appear to occur haphazardly:

Ex.53

Allegretto vivace

In what follows the oboe completes the alto tune, and then the chorus starts a double fugue on the word 'pacem' alone. The more important of the two subjects preserves the simple stepwise progress that Beethoven had wanted from the first:

Ex.54

It will be noticed that the upper theme rises in sequence. Because it sounds relaxed and untroubled it became very dear to Beethoven's heart in his last years. In two of the string quartets he wrote shortly before his death, the C sharp minor (first movement) and the F major (last movement), he worked these very same phrases in even crotchets the other way up, the sequences falling instead of rising. I shall return to this comparison later.

It is easy to go too far in pointing out such likenesses, where they are almost certainly due to coincidence. But the dividing line is hard to find and will be in different places for different people. It is probably coincidence that the stepwise 'peace' theme (Ex.54) has a rather similar outline to the one right at the beginning of the Kyrie which starts with the leap of a fourth, and it is probably coincidence that you can pick out this same outline in the lower of the two fugue subjects quoted above. But if it be agreed, as surely it must be, that Beethoven's mind was so imbued with certain ideas that he threw off likenesses unconsciously then the word coincidence ceases to have any precise meaning.

The fugato ends with one of Beethoven's favourite devices, more used in the music of his Middle Period than in his late works: a crescendo that leads not to a *forte* but to a sudden *piano*. In this case the crescendo dissolves into the most memorable four bars in the movement:

This phrase, sung here without any accompaniment, occurs four times in the course of the Dona, and each time one welcomes it for its marvellously consoling hopefulness. It starts as far as possible from the tonic without being in another key, and the finding of the tonic at the end seems to symbolize the finding of peace. The word Dona is now sung to a falling sixth which suggests a more urgent prayer than the falling third to which it was sung earlier (Ex.53).

There is certainly symbolism a few bars later with peace seeming to float down from heaven as our prayers rise:

New ideas now occur in profusion. After a repeat of the one just quoted there is another fugato, very brief, on what Riezler calls the germinal motive. The sudden *fortissimo* is unexpected:

Ex. 57

This leads to a climax of near-desperation as the chorus calls loudly for peace in alternation with quieter pleas from the four soloists. With the chorus stuck for eight bars on a chord of A major you think this must be the dominant leading to a return of D major and the music with which the Dona began. What it really leads to is completely unexpected and to account for it a digression is required.

In a small-scale Mass such as Britten's a quiet unassertive ending is satisfying and indeed desirable, but in so vast a conception as Beethoven's a quiet unassertive ending would risk anticlimax. Ethel Smyth could see no way of setting 'Dona nobis pacem' other than very quietly. Accordingly she recommended that in her Mass the Gloria should be performed not after the Kyrie but as a finale after the Agnus Dei, and she will have found support for this order in the Anglican Book of Common Prayer which in her day placed the Gloria near the end of the Communion Service.* In his Mass in C Beethoven had ended softly without any trace of anticlimax partly by intensifying his invention—this seems to me the most successful movement of the five—and partly because he was writing within modest limits for a church of modest dimensions. But the Missa Solemnis is cathedral music and Beethoven realized that a big climax was essential for the finale of such a work. The words seem quite alien to a big climax, but Beethoven found a way round this difficulty by borrowing an innovation he found in Haydn's *Missa in tempore belli*. Haydn had composed this work in 1796 when Napoleon's army was rampaging round Styria. The war must have seemed very close to those who lived in Vienna or Eisenstadt and heard the first performance of Haydn's Mass, and he had the notion of interpolating in the final prayer for peace passages that brought to mind the very war they were praying to avoid.

*Anglican Communion Services now have these words said near the start, as in Catholic churches.

Almost from the beginning of the Agnus Dei the timpani are rumbling ominously 'as if one heard the enemy approaching in the distance'—the words were written soon afterwards by some-one who had been in the congregation[1]—and we also hear occasional interjections by the trumpets in this very impressive movement. Then at the start of the Dona trumpets, woodwind and drums unite in a sudden *forte* explosion:

(The notes in brackets are omitted by the trumpets.) We hear these 'war' instruments only once more in the Dona; Haydn made little attempt to build a big climax as Beethoven was to do, but he had led up to this *forte* explosion with high originality; the timpani rhythm in bar 2 of the above occurs more than a dozen times in the course of the Adagio.

No war was troubling the Austrian Empire in the early 1820s but Beethoven must have had vivid memories of trying to compose the *Emperor* Concerto while Napoleon's cannon were bombarding Vienna. Central Europe had been ravaged by war for almost all his adult life, and it is not surprising that he should describe his music as a 'Prayer for inner and outer Peace'. He had been praying for outer peace, the avoidance of war, since the start of the Dona, but he wanted now to make the horrors of war more of a reality to his audience-congregation, as Haydn had done. At first war is no more than a distant danger, and to suggest distance he has his timpanist rumbling *pianissimo* on the lowest possible note, F. This makes the choice of B flat trumpets almost inevitable, F being the dominant of this key. The drumming will be the more dramatic if it sounds like an interruption and Beethoven organized this interruption with the same skill he had shown over the trumpet in *Fidelio*. The previous section, as was mentioned above, ended with a long-held chord of A. He eliminated all notes but A itself which, when the timpani roll starts on low F, becomes the third in a new and unexpected key. At the same time there has been a collapse from full tutti to near-silence and almost at once the timpani is the only instrument left playing. After nearly four bars the strings briefly but marvellously give a shudder of apprehension, and then *pianissimo* trumpets bring the danger a little nearer:

Ex.59

As will be seen, the trumpets are interrupted by a desperate cry from the alto soloist, not for peace but for mercy which Beethoven may well have thought should come first. The tenor soloist repeats this 'outcry of terrified humanity'[2] with heightened intensity, and the chorus dramatically interposes a single *forte* 'miserere nobis'. For a brief moment trumpets and drums are menacingly *fortissimo* but, high above, the soprano soloist is heard turning desperation back to an uncertain hope with a cry for help; the immediate danger passes and the prayer for peace and the D major themes heard earlier return.

This first war episode has taken many words to describe and it took Beethoven a great many pages in his sketch book, yet in performance it lasts not much more than half a minute. Its effect is out of all proportion to its length in seconds. Two tiny and almost irrelevant details: some of the drum roll sketches are labelled 'Marsch'; and since the 1960s there has been a tendency for the alto soloist to sing the first syllable of 'Dei' in the passage quoted above as a crotchet appoggiatura, one note higher than written. This was a recitative convention in the classical period, and though the 1820s seems rather late for it Beethoven may well have counted on it. An appoggiatura is more convincing in the alto's phrase than in the tenor's five bars later, but both are possible.

Beethoven now develops the falling thirds from Ex.53, repeats Ex.55 unaccompanied, and then embarks on a suddenly *fortissimo* fugato:

Ex.60

He probably thought he was developing the falling sixth the sopranos have just sung (Ex.55) and was presumably unconscious of nearly repeating the fugato in Handel's *Hallelujah* Chorus—'And he shall reign for ever and ever'. He is known to have studied and copied out several Handel choruses with a view to preparing himself for the composition of the Missa Solemnis, and this was surely one of them. But Handel would not have tied the quavers across the barlines in the countersubject.

In spite of a calm repetition of Ex.56 Beethoven now develops a driving energy that is almost too much for words (Ex.57 is prominent), and when he feels that the words are getting in his way he discards them and launches into a 60 bar passage for the orchestra alone:

Ex.61

These two tiny themes are worked in double counterpoint—with sometimes one as the bass and sometimes the other—and the very fast tempo and delicate scoring have the effect of a Scherzo. This is not what one expects in a Solemn Mass; the whole section is extremely puzzling. But as music it is immensely enjoyable, and Beethoven must have welcomed the chance he had contrived for himself to show his never-equalled skill at developing themes. Furthermore he needed music of some sort that would enable him to build up an overwhelming crescendo of energy at the centre of his finale, culminating in his second war episode. But his way of achieving this climax is like nothing else in religious music, and there has been a good deal of speculation as to how this Scherzo, if that is what it is, links on to the rest of the movement thematically and what, if anything, it represents.

The linking is more visual and intellectual than audible. The lower of the themes quoted above is the higher of the two in Ex.54 with the note lengths made even, but I doubt if any listener has ever noticed this unless he has first studied the score. Even then he will need to be sharp-eyed to appreciate the link, for quite apart from the difference in tempo and rhythm the moods are poles apart as well. The 'meaning' of this passage is at least as obscure. 'It is permissible', wrote Tovey, 'to interpret this as the change from prosperity to arrogance followed by its Nemesis',[3] by which he means the subsequent return of the war music, and he goes on to suggest that this section starts 'exultant' and ends 'alarmingly rough and wild'. Martin Cooper wrote that the passage 'carries the Missa Solemnis still further outside the boundaries of the liturgy and suggests the ordered activity, the bustle and inhumanity rather than the horror of war'.[4] Walter Riezler finds here 'the confusion of the world in general . . . [and] the chaos from which our longing for peace springs'. But to me this orchestral section suggests not so much prosperity, ordered activity, or chaos as a hectic indifference to the imminence of war, the ball in Brussels on the eve of Waterloo, the appalling cheerfulness of Chamberlain returning from Munich.

In the middle of this closely-developed Scherzo Beethoven inverts his stepwise theme and comes very close indeed to writing the finale of his last string quartet, the F major Op.135. I give a few bars from each work:

Ex.62

There is certainly something both 'rough and wild' and even 'chaotic' about the rapid key changes at the end of this orchestral episode. Suddenly it is interrupted by *fortissimo* violence on trumpets and drums with everyone else joining in. This is the climax of the movement, with war seemingly on the very doorstep. Once again the soprano soloist emerges from the holocaust holding a high A flat and leads the music once again from terror to hope.

In the final section D major is restored and most of the peace themes recur. As a coda there are distant timpani rumblings, this time on B flat, and with the trumpets silent we sense that the danger of war is diminishing, especially as the rumbles alternate with echoes of Ex.55—bars 3 and 4 only. The quiet repetitions of these two bars by either chorus or woodwind have an almost elegiac beauty which anticipates Mahler's repetition of 'ewig' at the end of *Das Lied von der Erde*. Ex.56 returns with peace floating down from heaven on the horns, and the violins are just beginning to float down too when they are magically interrupted by the chorus singing Ex.55 for the last time. This final section is supremely beautiful except perhaps for the last four loud bars for the orchestra alone which seem to me rather perfunctory. Tovey is kinder than I am about them, writing of 'chords of innocent triumph'.

Like the finale of the Ninth Symphony, Beethoven's Agnus Dei has been subjected to far more adverse criticism than all the other movements put together. Even Martin Cooper who writes with such sympathy and understanding of Beethoven's late music feels that, like the Benedictus, the Agnus Dei does not 'quite sustain the sublime power and simplicity of the earlier movements. The battle-scenes . . . are not on a level of inspiration with the serene magnificence and classical proportions of the Kyrie.'[5] Riezler quotes one Walter Krug as calling these war episodes

Beethoven's 'worst error of judgment'. Objections to them were being voiced almost from the first, even by Schindler.

The whole work would be improved if. . . the dramatic section of the Dona that many justifiably find so offensive were omitted. If there is no feasible way to cross over the wide, though divided, stream, the crossing must be effected at the expense of a few beautiful moments. One could well skip from the second bar on page 252 of the score to the first bar on page 289 where the full chorus and orchestra enter with a marvellous D major section and carry the movement to its conclusion. This advice is not intended for fanatical Beethovenians. . .[6]

This cut, say Schindler's editors, is puzzling, for if he is referring to the original Schott score (and it seems there was then no other) it makes no sense. Presumably Schindler meant a cut from bar 163 (immediately before the first *pianissimo* drum roll) to bar 359 (the return to D major after the second war episode) but it is hard to believe that anyone in his senses would regard such a cut as an improvement. Complaints about the two war episodes stem in part from the belief commonly held in the past that what is theatrical must be at odds with what is religious, in spite of the fact that the Mass itself was theatrical in origin, with the priest representing Christ at the Last Supper and the congregation representing the Apostles. It will not have escaped notice that I profoundly disagree with adverse criticisms of this movement. To me the war episodes are neither trivial as music nor unsuited to a religious work. Indeed they provide the Agnus Dei with just that climax it would not otherwise have had, just that climax which it needs as the finale of so profound a work. So far from being undesirable in the Dona, reminders of war and its horrors give it a reality that makes most other settings of these words sound superficial by comparison.

Though the Agnus Dei is much easier to sing than the Gloria or Credo, it is, I believe, more difficult to conduct. The music must have an inevitability which will impress the listener only if the conductor himself believes in it. The Agnus Dei will then make a marvellously satisfying end to this very great work.

9

The Orchestration of the Missa Solemnis

Beethoven was the only great composer who, in his later years, was not able to improve his major works after the first run-through; the reason being, of course, that he could not hear the run-through. It is almost impossible for a composer to assess down to the last detail what orchestral music will sound like. Even such sharp-eared and experienced composer-conductors as Mendelssohn and Mahler made countless alterations after the first run-through of their masterpieces, and Mahler made as many again after the second, third and fourth. Beethoven could not do this, and the denial of a second chance meant that he could not improve passages in which the balance was faulty (as for instance in the second subject to the Ninth Symphony Scherzo), and probably meant that on occasions he did not risk experiments of which he could never judge the effect. His deafness may also account for a certain clumsiness in the scoring here and there, the texture thickened at climaxes in a rather haphazard way as for instance early on in the Credo: bars 20 to 30 seem to me clumsy in a way you never find in the Mass in C.

As a young man Beethoven had been an orchestral violinist and he knew that music had to be made interesting to play as well as to hear. His string writing in the Missa Solemnis shows plenty of evidence of this awareness. Though he sometimes has his strings doubling the chorus (which is boring for the players), he often writes a vigorous kind of near-doubling which is much more interesting. Compare the first violins and the sopranos in this fugato entry from the Gloria (bar 90 *ff*):

Ex.63

The discords pass us by so quickly that we are hardly aware of them, but they do add a relish to the sound and violinists will enjoy playing such bars much more than if they were given the simple crotchets of the voice part. Beethoven had probably noticed such writing in Haydn's *Creation*, for instance some 30 bars from the end of Part 1, and he was surely influenced by the vigorous semiquavers Haydn gave his violinists in the *Nelson Mass*—notably in the Kyrie and towards the end of the Credo—semiquavers that are often a decoration of the much simpler soprano line. But Beethoven has a higher proportion of discords than Haydn. Another example can be found in the fugue subject of the 'Osanna'.

Beethoven's consideration for his players extends to the lower strings. Here are the violas and cellos filling in the fugue subject of the 'Pleni sunt coeli':

Ex.64

Beethoven sometimes gives his cellists interesting parts even when there is little chance of their being heard, as for instance in the 'et homo factus est' section of the Credo (bar 149 *ff*):

Ex.65

There is a similarly interesting but inaudible bassoon part in the Dona immediately after the first war episode (bar 196–211).

It is remarkable how often Beethoven suppresses the violins in both the Missa Solemnis and in the Ninth Symphony. In the choral finale of the symphony they play in only 17 of the first 138 bars, and in only 8 of the first 83 in the six-eight variation in B flat. Here Beethoven leaves out the strings because he is imitating a military band but he can have had no such purpose in the later slow section sometimes sung to the words 'O ye millions'. In the Missa Solemnis the violins do not play in the first section of the Credo fugue, in the Sanctus or in the Prae-ludium, and it is significant that at this very time Beethoven was thinking of writing yet another Mass with no strings at all.* There is much to be said for giving the various sections of an orchestra a breather in the course of a long and difficult work; nineteenth century opera composers often did this and perhaps would have forfeited the affection of their players if they hadn't. But Beethoven is not nearly so kind to his lower strings, and at times shows what looks almost like malice towards his bassoons and trombones. This was due to the habit common among the great classical composers of marking these parts 'Col Bassi' and not bothering to write them out. The copyist, finding no notes on the bassoon stave, wrote into the bassoon part what the composer had given to the cellos, and often the composer never thought of the effect of these notes on a wind instrument. The bassoons and double bassoon have a torrid time of it at the start of Beethoven's Gloria, the double bassoon playing almost contin-uous quick quavers for the first 42 bars without any chance whatsoever of taking breath. Not that it matters, for with so much going on no one will notice if notes are omitted.

In gentle music Beethoven often leaves out the oboes, feeling no doubt that their slightly astringent tone prevents their blending smoothly enough with the other woodwind. They do not play in the first section of the Credo fugue, in the Sanctus or in the Benedictus apart from half a dozen fairly loud bars near the end. Hereabouts the flutes are silent for even longer. After their descent from heaven at the very start of the Benedictus they are not heard again for nearly 20 minutes—until well on in the Agnus Dei. Again Beethoven is less concerned about resting the lower instruments. The bassoons have far fewer rests than the flutes, oboes or clarinets. But in quiet music he uses them with high imagination—to convey deep melancholy at the start of the Agnus Dei and to heighten tragedy in the Credo (Ex.32). Oboe

*See pp.21–2.

and bassoon marvellously intensify despair in the Gloria (Ex.12); flute and clarinet are preferred for consolation.

His writing for the horns is a strange mixture of Ancient and Modern. It is generally though not invariably believed that the valve horn was not available in time for Beethoven's concert in 1824. According to Morley Pegge the first work by a well-known composer which was quite definitely written for a valve-horn was Schubert's song with horn obbligato, *Auf dem Strom* (1828). For years, horn concertos such as Mozart's had required soloists to play the notes in between the harmonic series and to disguise their poor quality as best they could, but Mozart did not expect orchestral horn players to produce such notes. Beethoven was a little more adventurous; even so the famous passage he wrote for the Fourth Horn in the slow movement of the Ninth Symphony (bars 83-98) is astonishing. As well as exploring the extremes of the instrument's range the part includes notes never normally written in orchestral music including a quickish written scale of A flat. In his book about the horn Horace Fitzpatrick argues that these bars are perfectly playable on the natural horn, and indeed he plays them himself on the record that goes with the book.[1] There might seem to be no arguing with this but at least some comments are called for. If such an exceptionally gifted player was on hand in Vienna why did Beethoven, Schubert and others not write for him like this in other works? Above all, why did Beethoven give these spectacular difficulties to the Fourth Horn instead of to the First? I cannot find that anyone has considered this point. If such a part in a new work were given to the Fourth Horn in a modern symphony orchestra the First Horn would threaten to resign. It does seem to me probable that Beethoven had been told of a young and adventurous player with a valve-horn in Vienna, that this instrument was not favoured by Vienna's older and more conservative hornists, and that in spite of them Beethoven decided to try it out.

If so, he heard of this player too late to write adventurously in the Missa Solemnis. Indeed some of the horn writing suggests that Beethoven was still living in the eighteenth century. Consider the way the horn doubles the oboe in the Kyrie: (see Ex.66). This selective doubling is attractive and subtle, and it can be argued that Beethoven, thinking the horn's high notes too obtrusive in such gentle music, is making a virtue of necessity in

Ex.66

omitting them. In fact they are easier and lower than some of those he asks his Fourth Horn to play *dolce* in the famous Ninth Symphony variation—which is *pianissimo* throughout. Also the missing notes turn up elsewhere in the Missa Solemnis (for instance in the Gloria bars 110–11), and there can hardly have been subtlety behind the selective doubling in the 'Osanna' fugue:

Ex.67

In this and other such doubling passages in the Missa Solemnis, the horn notes Beethoven omits are always those he had been taught to omit in his youth, and it would seem that in the 1820s he sometimes remembered and sometimes forgot recent improvements in the playing of the natural horn.

There is some evidence that Beethoven's horn writing becomes more adventurous towards the end of the Missa Solemnis. In the Sanctus the Second Horn has to play a number of D flats, E flats and B flats, as also a low F, and similar notes can be found later in the 'Pleni sunt coeli' and 'Osanna'. The odd thing is that throughout these three sections the First Horn does not play at all. It is almost as though in both the Ninth Symphony and in the Missa Solemnis Beethoven was carrying on a vendetta with his First Horn player; which can hardly be so because when he wrote these works he cannot have known what horn player would take part in the first performance. But there must be some explanation for his silencing Corno I. Quite exceptionally he wrote a low E flat in the Credo (bar 156) but it is the Second Horn who plays it.

On the evidence of the Missa Solemnis Beethoven expected his horn players to be able to change crooks quickly but not his trumpeters. Between the Agnus Dei and the Dona the horn players have five bars of rests in which to change from an E flat to a D crook, yet he never asks his trumpeters to change crooks in this movement. The result is that in the last part of the Dona they contribute very little to the overall effect because E (sounding D) is the only note in the D major scale that could be expected on a natural trumpet in B flat, and they play it a great many times. Yet faced with precisely the same problem in the finale of the Ninth Symphony Beethoven made his Second Trumpet change crooks from D to B flat and then back to D. Why did he not do the same in the Missa Solemnis? Beethoven's trumpet parts are usually dull and those in the Missa Solemnis are no exception (apart from the war episodes).

In the so-called Minuet of his First Symphony Beethoven had managed to write a few bars for the timpani which at a fast tempo are virtually unplayable. He was not deaf when he wrote this work, and you would expect the timpanist to have taken him aside after the performance and mentioned the difficulty. Yet in the third bar of the Gloria Beethoven did it again:

Ex. 68

Allegro vivace

If the reader thinks this looks easy he should take a pencil in each hand, imagine two timpani in front of him, and see how he gets on. There is similarly awkward timpani writing in what I have called the second war episode in the Agnus Dei. Throughout the greater part of the Missa Solemnis the timpani and the trumpets play the same notes in the same rhythm, as they do in most works of the classical period.

Beethoven had written for trombones towards the end of his Fifth and Sixth Symphonies, in *Fidelio* and some of its overtures, in the slow introduction to his *Consecration of the House* and very occasionally in other works, but though the trombone writing in the Benedictus of the Missa Solemnis is imaginative he was more than a little handicapped in developing his understanding of this instrument. More go-ahead trombone writing can be found in Schubert's 'Great' C major Symphony written within two or three years of the Missa Solemnis. About the time when Beethoven became deaf the playing of this instrument was improving and it was being increasingly used in operas by such composers as Rossini and Weber. Schubert heard these operas and Beethoven did not. As we have seen* most of the trombone parts in the Missa Solemnis were added only after the completion of the autograph score and not by Beethoven, though under his instructions.

The last-minute addition of trombones in Masses and Oratorios derived from a rather casual tradition about which Beethoven may have learnt as a boy. An uncertain chorus could be given confidence if the three trombones doubled the altos, tenors and basses. Mozart hardly ever scored positively for trombones in the numerous Masses he composed in his Salzburg days,[2] perhaps because he could trust his singers, but copyists quite often added doubling parts for these instruments in choruses, sometimes at his request but more often on their own initiative. No doubt the players were used to adapting or omitting notes when unreasonable difficulties arose, and as we have seen they did sometimes arise in the Missa Solemnis when Beethoven did not check what his copyists had done with sufficient care. He was not the only composer of whom this could be said. In *The Creation* Haydn took a great deal of care about the trombone parts in most of the choruses, but in the penultimate chorus in Part 2 his attention must have wandered; he asked that the bass trombone and double bassoon should double the Bassi line and because he did not himself write out their parts he never noticed that they were unplayable.

The published full score of the Missa Solemnis contains an organ part which does not occur in the autograph because it too was added at the last moment. Beethoven never wrote it out. He merely indicated to his copyist which passages should be marked 'Org.' and include doubling notes in the right hand, and which should be marked 'senza org.' and consist only of a bass line.

*See p.48.

The part is of little interest, and its omission in performances need not be regretted.

Beethoven told Schotts the order he wanted for the instrumental and vocal staves in the published full score, and they appear in that order in the Eulenburg score. In as many as three letters he promised to send metronome markings for the Missa Solemnis in the immediate future but he never did. His reasons for not so doing were 'business affairs'; he was too busy correcting the proofs of his late string quartets, and he was 'just about to undergo a fourth operation'. This last letter was written for him by Schindler on 22 February 1827; Beethoven signed it. Just over a month later he died.

10
Since Beethoven's Death

In no country has the Missa Solemnis found an easy success since its composer's death, and though the chief reason for its neglect is its difficulty there are other reasons as well. All are on the decline, though none that I shall mention has yet vanished from view.

To begin with, a good orchestral work will always receive many more performances than an equally good choral work. Choruses are not always popular with leading conductors because until the last moment their training has to be left to others and the last moment is usually too late to make significant changes. They also tend to be unpopular with orchestras; players dislike feeling they are no longer the centre of attention, and they dislike even more having to scrape and blow inaudibly because of the noise the singers are making. Furthermore choral concerts take much more organizing than orchestral concerts.

In many countries Masses and Requiems used to suffer from an almost insurmountable handicap owing to the nature of their Latin words. Apart from the fact that to most people such words are incomprehensible, Catholics used to feel it was improper to sing them in a concert-hall, and Low-Church Protestants often felt it was improper to sing them at all. In Victorian times it seemed quite intolerable that Masses should be sung in a Protestant Cathedral, and at Three Choirs Festivals they were invariably advertised (on the rare occasions when they were performed) as 'Services', and sung to innocuous English words that bore little or no relationship to the Latin. Even so there were often protests from those who saw through this disguise and felt that the Devil was come among them. Of a Gloucester performance of Beethoven's Mass in C in 1850 the *Illustrated London News* reported that 'there was a considerable secession from the auditory, marking painfully the schism in the High and

Low Church', those who 'seceded' being, needless to add, of the Low Church persuasion. As late as the 1880s a Mass could be performed in London's Exeter Hall only if it were called a Service and sung in English. In the first half of our own century Masses were performed no more often at Three Choirs Festivals than they had been in Victorian times, and that was very seldom indeed. There are still those who think very seldom is too often.

By the 1850s and perhaps earlier 'R.G. Loraine Esq' (as he liked to be called on the title-page) was at work trying to make Novello's vocal scores of Masses acceptable to non-Catholics. No single set of English words would fit every Mass so he made several, and often achieved near-nonsense in the process. Haydn, trying in his *Nelson* Mass to instil sincerity and fervour into his setting of 'Credo in unum Deum, Patrem omnipotentem', would not much have liked hearing the result sung to 'Lord, thou hast made mine enemies also to turn their backs on me', and Beethoven would have despaired at hearing the symbolism of his music for 'Et resurrexit tertia die, secundum scripturas' in his C major Mass obliterated by the words 'Be thou exalted, O Lord, in thine own strength'. R.G. Loraine may also have tried his hand at the Missa Solemnis but I have not found evidence that he did. The fact that this work was not sung at a Three Choirs Festival until 1880—and only once more before 1909—may mean that no English text was available.

In England the music was first heard in curious circumstances on Christmas Eve 1832, in Queen Square London, at the house of a Mr Alsager. Thomas Massa Alsager (1779–1846) merits a digression because he made a notable contribution to the Arts in England, yet they never found room for him in the *Dictionary of National Biography*. His first contribution was fortuitous: he bought a book. It was an old book by George Chapman and dated 1616, and he lent it to his friend Charles Cowden Clarke. Clarke was friendly with Keats who had been at his father's school in Edmonton, and at supper in the autumn of 1816 he showed him the book. Keats read it straight through from cover to cover, walked home at dawn making up a sonnet, wrote the sonnet down and got a messenger to take the result back to Cowden Clarke who found it on his breakfast table that same morning. It was, of course, 'On first looking into Chapman's Homer'.

Alsager was a good friend to Leigh Hunt, visited him in prison and put him up when he was released. Charles Lamb was struck by Alsager's imperturbability; 'he is proof against weather, ingratitude and meat under-done'.[1] When he stayed with the Wordsworths at Rydal Mount, Joanna Monkhouse, Wordsworth's sister-in-law and rising thirty-seven, was in grave danger of losing her heart to him,[2] but he married someone else and soon produced a family. He had been City Correspondent of *The Times* since 1817 and probably wrote music criticism for the paper as well though it seems he was never, as has sometimes been said, the editor. But he did become one of the proprietors and he arranged for *The Times* to employ a full-time music critic; it was the first London paper to do so. Alsager himself played the violin and, after a fashion, most of the other instruments of the orchestra. His last venture into the Arts was to set up chamber music classes and concerts in Harley Street. At the 1845 concerts all the Beethoven quartets were played, and this seems to have been the first time that the late quartets were heard in London.

By the 1830s Alsager had started a concert society which gave performances in his own house in Queen Square, Bloomsbury. Beethoven was his favourite composer but the programmes often included works by other composers as well. In 1834 a Cherubini Requiem, presumably the D minor, had its first performance in England and a little later Spohr conducted.[3] Alsager was quick to buy a full score of the Missa Solemnis and he got his concert secretary, a cellist named Grimal, to persuade Ignaz Moscheles to conduct it. Moscheles, a brilliant pianist and a fair composer, had known Beethoven in Vienna and often dined out on their friendship.[4] He became 'completely absorbed in that colossal work', as he later put it in his autobiography, though he had doubts about certain details.

The Fitzwilliam Museum in Cambridge has a copy of the programme which names all the performers.[5] A surprising number were notable. The soloists included Clara Novello (soprano) and Alfred Novello (bass). Clara was to become famous all over Western Europe but when she first fought her way through Beethoven's appalling difficulties she was only fourteen. Her brother Alfred was twenty-two and already on the ladder that was to take him to the top in London music publishing. Their father,

Vincent Novello, played the organ at this performance and their elder sister Mary, who was Mrs Cowden Clarke, and their brother Edward sang in the chorus as did Charles Cowden Clarke himself. Edward Holmes (1797–1859) who had been at the Clarke school at the same time as Keats, sang tenor in the chorus. As a youth he had studied and lodged with Vincent Novello, and his recent *Ramble among the Musicians of Germany* is still worth reading as are some of the music criticisms he had been writing in the *Atlas*. But he is best remembered today for his admirable *Life of Mozart* (1845) which until quite recently was available in the Everyman Edition. We shall meet him again later in this chapter.

The orchestra in the Alsager home included all the instruments demanded by the score except the double bassoon, but the strings were few in number: 3–2–2–2–2. No doubt they were limited by lack of space as was the chorus; 3–4–7–5. This imbalance will have resulted fortuitously from the abilities of those the Alsagers and Novellos knew and felt able to invite. Mrs Cowden Clarke sustained the alto line supported only by three choirboys, one of whom seems to have been E.J. Hopkins, later a composer of popular hymn tunes and chants. 'The enthusiasm of my English friends fired me,' wrote Moscheles later; 'the Benedictus, with its heavenly violin solo (Mori) enchanted us all.' His memory must have betrayed him for Mori is not mentioned in the programme which names the Belgian, Tolbecque, as leader of the first violins. A pupil of Kreutzer, he played in the band at His Majesty's Theatre. The Benedictus, it may be remembered, had also been especially popular in St Petersburg; one would expect early audiences to prefer it to the other movements.

The first public performances of the Missa Solemnis in London were conducted by Vincent Novello at the London Tavern on both 1 April 1839 and 1 April 1840, and again his daughter Clara was the soprano soloist. They probably left out the Credo as they probably did at the Queen Square performance; the Missa Solemnis was not heard complete in London until 1870. Things were not much better in Germany and Austria. Zelter's Singakademie in Berlin which had given the famous though much cut performance of the St Matthew Passion under Mendelssohn in 1829, gave an even more drastically cut version of the Missa Solemnis in 1834; only the Kyrie and Gloria were attempted. I am uncertain as to the date of the first complete performance in Germany or Austria, and suspect that cuts were made in Reichenberg in 1832, in Pressbourg as part of High Mass in 1835 and in Dresden in 1839 because these performances are not mentioned by Schindler.[6] He cites as the first complete performance anywhere the one conducted by Spohr at Bonn in 1845, and knew of no others before those at Cologne and Frankfurt in 1855. The first complete liturgical performance was, he thought, the one on 4 August 1857 in the Freiburg Cathedral at Baden.

The *Musical Times* sent a critic to the Bonn performance of 1845, and he was almost certainly Edward Holmes.

In England, at this day, the Missa Solemnis is as completely unknown as on the day it was published. The Germans, however, have mastered it; and the performance on the 10th of August displayed it in all its grandeur and beauty... The time will come (though I shall not live to see it) when the Missa Solemnis of Beethoven will be regarded as we now regard the great works of Handel.[7]

I shall not live to see it either, but I hope he was right. Spohr, the conductor at Bonn, was not in fact an admirer of Beethoven's late works. Schindler thought the surprising excellence of the performance was mainly due to the careful rehearsing of the singers by Franz Weber, the royal music director at Cologne.

In the nineteenth century concerts with orchestras were such a rarity outside the great cities that most people got to know Beethoven symphonies through piano duet arrangements they played in their own homes. As early as 1829 Czerny arranged Beethoven's Mass in C as a piano duet, and in 1859 the Missa Solemnis was similarly arranged by Nottebohm, who later studied and wrote about Beethoven's sketch books. In the late 1830s excerpts from the Missa Solemnis were published in London in vocal scores edited by Vincent Novello. The British Library has the Kyrie and also 'Grand Quartet & Chorus, Quoniam tu solus sanctus', which in fact runs to the end of the Gloria and includes the fugue. Both title-pages state that the music is 'as performed at the York Music Festivals etc.', and the conclusion is inescapable that there was at least one public performance in York before those conducted by Vincent Novello in London. A complete vocal score was published for a guinea by Novellos early in 1846,[8] and made possible Costa's 'Philharmonic' performance in London on 16 March*, as also a 'wretchedly mutilated' one in Birmingham that July.

Masses did better in England than they might have done because of the Novellos being practising Catholics. By the time Vincent retired in 1849, his son Alfred had in effect been running the firm for some years. Almost at once he took the bold step of halving the selling price of vocal scores and publishing a large number of others very cheaply. This made possible the proliferation of choral societies all over Britain in the second half of the century. Bolstered by the money they were making out of *Messiah*, *The Creation* and *Elijah*, and inspired by Catholic ambitions, Novellos risked bringing out cheap vocal scores of numerous Masses by Haydn, Mozart and Beethoven, and most of them included by way of foreword a detailed and intelligent analysis of the music by Edward Holmes; these analyses had originally appeared in the *Musical Times*, the periodical that Novellos had founded in 1844. They even published all six of Schubert's Masses, three by Hummel and both of Weber's; in these cases the English words were not laid under the Latin but appeared in a quite separate vocal score described as Communion Service. The Latin versions were cheaper than the English; even so they can have sold very few copies. Most Victorians saw little reason to buy Popish music when *Messiah* and *Elijah* were available. I have traced very few performances of these Masses.

The remarkable thing is that the Missa Solemnis fared no better. What seems to have been the first complete performance in Britain was the one in London conducted by Joseph Barnby in March 1870 'without curtailment or alteration' and, puzzlingly, 'not with the inverted passages for the voices used elsewhere'.[9] Sir Charles Hallé gave the first performance in Manchester on 2 March 1871 and this too must have been complete. The choir, reported the *Guardian* critic, 'at times showed symptoms of exhaustion', and no wonder, he thought, for the work was 'less singable than anything else in existence. To the majority of the audience the performance was wearisome.' However Hallé repeated it more than most conductors—at

*See p.78.

roughly ten-yearly intervals—and in July 1882 he conducted a performance in London of which the *Musical Times* wrote 'To speak plain truth, the work is impossible. No human lungs can endure the strain imposed by it, nor can human energy and skill do more than approximate to a perfect execution. Mr Hallé's chorus was fairly beaten by some passages'.[10] It would not be unreasonable to say that most choruses have been fairly beaten by them ever since. Bernard Shaw, in his capacity as the music critic Corno di Bassetto, wrote of the equally difficult Choral Symphony: 'I am prepared to face the transposition of the choral section a semitone down rather than have it marred by tearing and straining at impossibilities.' He would probably have advocated the same solution of the Missa Solemnis problems but I have not heard of its being tried nor would it solve anything. Difficulty gives difficult music part of its quality. Beethoven's *Grosse Fuge* can be played with much less strain by a string orchestra but strain contributes to the effect of a good string quartet performance. Since the last war choral societies all over Europe have become far more skilful than they ever were before it, and the best of them no longer sound fairly beaten by the Credo, though one still senses here and there a struggle against tremendous odds, as (in my view) one should.

But if the Missa Solemnis is at last becoming comparatively well-known, it has achieved this position only recently. In his *Mirror of Music* Percy Scholes compiled some statistics[11] from reviews in the *Musical Times** and these show that whereas in the winter of 1886–87 England managed to mount just one performance of each Beethoven Mass, there were five performances of Gounod's *Messe Solennelle*, 22 of *Elijah* and 64 of *Messiah*. Forty years later in 1926-27 Bach's B minor Mass had gone up from one to eight but the Missa Solemnis only from one to two, with 20 for *Elijah* and 46 for *Messiah*. Watkins Shaw has compiled statistics for the Three Choirs Festivals and shown that in the hundred years up to 1953 only one Mass by Haydn was performed (the *Nelson* in 1879 and 1953); only one by Schubert, the E flat in 1887; one by Hummel, the E flat in 1872; none by Mozart except for the spurious 'Twelfth Mass' which was astonishingly popular in the 1850s and 60s (and earlier).

---

*It must be remembered that not all performances were reviewed.

Apart from the Haydn in 1953 all these were sung to English words, as was Beethoven's Mass in C (three performances, all before 1900). The Missa Solemnis achieved as many as four performances, the same number as Cherubini's huge Mass in D minor, but incredibly none of these was given in the last 25 years, that is between 1928 and 1953. Against these dismal figures can be set around 90 performances of both *Messiah* and *Elijah* and even Spohr's *Last Judgment* notched about 30 in Victoria's reign.

Perhaps 1926–27 was an unlucky year for Scholes to have picked on so far as the Missa Solemnis is concerned, for in fact things were looking up by then, mainly due in England to the advocacy of Sir Hugh Allen. He was appointed conductor of the London Bach Choir in 1907 and throughout the 1920s he conducted the Oxford Bach Choir as well. Bach's B minor Mass and the Missa Solemnis were his favourite works and he did more than anyone in England to make concert-goers aware of their greatness. And indeed chorus singers. Those he rehearsed and conducted in the Missa Solemnis had an experience to treasure all their lives. Today there are several conductors of whom as much might be said, Klemperer and Giulini for instance, and the Gramophone Catalogue bears witness to an ever-widening appreciation of the Missa Solemnis, an appreciation that was only in its infancy before the war and was virtually non-existent in Victorian times.

A work so seldom performed in the nineteenth century could not then have had much influence on composers. The great Romantics were influenced in the main not by the music of Beethoven's Third Period but by what he wrote in his Early and Middle Periods, and Bartók was probably the first to be more affected by the later works. No one can say with certainty what a great composer never heard, but it would be unsurprising if, for instance, Mendelssohn, Berlioz and Tchaikovsky never heard the Missa Solemnis, at least in its complete form. (At one time Mendelssohn owned one of the Missa Solemnis sketch-books; with hardly credible generosity he gave it to Moscheles.) Schubert may well have attended the concert in Vienna at which parts of the Missa Solemnis were heard for the first time in Western Europe, for on 31 March 1824 he wrote to a friend in anticipation of it.[12] The full score had been available for more than a year when in July 1828 Schubert wrote, perhaps too quickly, his last

Mass, the one in E flat. Less characteristic than the A flat, it nevertheless has some fine moments, and in one or two it is possible to suspect Beethoven's influence. These bars from the Kyrie show Schubert tying crotchets across the barline in a Beethovenish way:

This passage can be compared with one in Beethoven's Gloria (bar 220 *ff*):

though Schubert's long-held pedal note is at the bottom of the harmony and Beethoven's at the top. A rather similar rhythm can be found near the beginning of Schubert's Agnus Dei.

It has recently been suggested* that Brahms was quoting the opening theme of Beethoven's Credo in his Third Symphony at bar 187 of the first movement:

*by Bernard Keeffe in a TV programme.

Ex. 71

The fact that these bars are unrelated thematically to anything else in the movement makes it the more likely that they have an extra-musical or even autobiographical significance. There are certainly autobiographical implications elsewhere, notably in the first two bars where the F-A-F motto theme stands for 'Frei aber froh' and in bars 3 and 4 which contain a quotation from Schumann's Third Symphony (first movement, bar 449 *ff*). Just why Brahms should quote Schumann's symphony and Beethoven's Credo in this movement will never be known, but his close friendship with Clara must have taught him that Schumann himself often included quotations in his music, in many cases so closely disguised that they remained unnoticed until recently. One would expect his pupil Brahms sometimes to adopt the same methods.

Though the war music in Beethoven's Agnus Dei has come in for adverse criticism in some quarters it certainly impressed Vaughan Williams and influenced his *Dona nobis pacem* for chorus and orchestra. Written in the mid-1930s when war with Germany seemed inevitable, this cantata begins with a short setting of the Agnus Dei words, but before the soprano soloist has finished singing, very softly, 'dona nobis pacem', the drums of war are heard as it were in the distance, and they rumble ever louder as brass fanfares lead to a harsh *fortissimo* setting for chorus of Walt Whitman's 'Beat! beat! drums!—blow! bugles! blow!'. The composer's purpose was precisely the same as Beethoven's—to demonstrate just what it was we were praying to be spared. After several more Whitman poems and settings of words from other sources the cantata ends very quietly with a repetition of 'dona nobis pacem'.

The only large-scale choral work I know that shows Beethoven's influence almost all through is the fine Mass that Ethel Smyth wrote in 1893 in the Missa Solemnis key of D. Tovey pointed out that 'in no single point is the treatment of the text similar. Yet in listening to either Mass the text seems to be treated in the only possible way: impressively, with tremendous emphasis; but without trace of eccentricity or paradox'.[13] At its best Ethel Smyth's music glows with a Beethoven-like vision, but she had assimilated her model and the influence is not easy to demonstrate. This is yet another Mass that is shamefully neglected.

But Beethoven's Missa Solemnis now receives more performances every year. And about time too if, as Charles Rosen has written, it is 'perhaps Beethoven's most considerable single achievement'.[14] This opinion, indeed, was held by Beethoven himself. As Edward Schulz reported after visiting him in September 1823, 'His second Mass he looks upon as his best work'.[15]

Notes

1: THE MASS IN BEETHOVEN'S DAY

1 From *Spectrum Charitatis* as translated early in the 17th century by William Prynne. Quoted by Terry.
2 *New Oxford History of Music* (Olleson) VII, p.306.
3 Landon, *Haydn 1801–1809*, pp.280-1. See also *Haydn, The Correspondence of*, p.234.
4 The autographs of Haydn 7 and 8 are both dated 1796; Landon now thinks 8 was performed first (*Haydn 1796–1800*, p.104). Haydn 9 was first performed not in the Bergkirche but in Eisenstadt Parish Church (*Haydn 1796–1800*, p.327). The reason for the late publication of Haydn 10 is not known. Hummel claimed to have written five masses for Eisenstadt; one in D minor (later published by Novello) was modelled on Haydn 9 in the same key. At this period the Prince also commissioned masses from Johann Fuchs (one of his employees), from Albrechtsberger and from Adalbert Gyrowetz. See Landon, *Haydn 1796–1800*, p.42, etc.
5 Schindler, pp.378-9.
6 Thayer, pp.1064-70.
7 In 8, 10 and 12 Haydn began his slow section earlier, at 'Gratias agimus'.
8 But it does not in Haydn 10, Hummel's B flat Mass and the Missa Solemnis.

2: THE MISSA SOLEMNIS COMPOSED AND PERFORMED

1 He also received the dedication of Schubert's Piano Sonata in A minor, Op.42.
2 *Letters of Beethoven*, pp.814-15 (only undated letters appear in these Notes).
3 Schindler, p.228.
4 Cooper, pp.43-5 for further details about Beethoven's complex bargaining with Simrock.
5 Thayer, p.854.
6 Thayer, p.840.

7 Schindler, pp.249-51.
8 *Letters of Beethoven*, p.1119 (augmentation of strings).
9 *Letters of Beethoven*, p.1122.
10 Schindler, p.283.
11 *Letters of Beethoven*, p.1124.
12 Thayer, p.925.

3: BEETHOVEN AS A CHRISTIAN

1 Thayer, p.820; Tovey, p.163; Robertson, *The Gramophone*, June 1953.
2 Schindler, p.365.
3 Thayer, pp.480-1.
4 Schindler, pp.365 and 390-1; facsimiles have been published.
5 Thayer, p.715.
6 Rosen, p.373; Robertson, *The Gramophone*, June 1953.

4: KYRIE

1 Tovey, p.166.
2 Riezler, p.190.
3 Thayer, p.720.

5: GLORIA

1 Bars 180-85 (deriving from 147-50).
2 At quite a late stage the tempo of the fugue was to have been Allegro maestoso e moderato; see Beethoven's letter of 13.12.23 to Prince Galitzin.
3 See early Augener edition of '48', 'Edited and Revised by Carl Czerny'.
4 Thayer, p.870.
5 Cooper, pp.172 and 238.

6: CREDO

1 Tovey, p.172.
2 Landon, *Haydn 1801-1809*, p.206.
3 Schindler, p.229. But he surely has either the wrong date or the wrong fugue. In August 1819 Beethoven would much more probably have been writing the fugue of the Gloria. Perhaps the visit took place a year later in August 1820. In his late masterpiece *Dr Faustus* Thomas Mann embroidered Schindler's description, attributing it to his young organist-composer, Kretschmar.
4 Rosen, p.375.

7: SANCTUS AND BENEDICTUS

1 Schindler, p.288.
2 Tovey, p.181.

8: AGNUS DEI

1 Landon, *Haydn 1796–1800*, pp.174-5; he is quoting G.A.von Grie-singer's *Biographische Notizen über Joseph Haydn*, 1810.
2 Hess, Foreword to the Eulenburg score.
3 Tovey, p.184.
4 Cooper, p.272.
5 Cooper, p.273.
6 Schindler, pp.285 and 350-1.

9: THE ORCHESTRATION OF THE MISSA SOLEMNIS

1 Horace Fitzpatrick, *The Horn and Horn Playing*, London, 1970, p.183.
2 But he did in the C minor Mass and the Requiem.

10: AFTER BEETHOVEN'S DEATH

1 *Letters of Charles and Mary Lamb*, Everyman Ed., i, p.367 and ii, p.139.
2 *Letters of Sarah Hutchinson*, ed. Coburn, London, 1954, p.111.
3 *Grove's Dictionary of Music and Musicians*, 1st ed., article on Alsager.
4 But see Schindler, pp.373-4 for a different view of this friendship.
5 Reproduced in the *Musical Times*, April 1902. My thanks to John Reed for this and other information used in this chapter.
6 Schindler, p.351. I owe this information to an editorial footnote by McArdle. See also pp.289-90.
7 Scholes, p.76.
8 *A Century and a Half in Soho*, p.50.
9 Scholes, p.31.
10 Scholes, p.78.
11 Scholes, p.144.
12 O.E.Deutsch, *Schubert, A Documentary Biography*, p.339.
13 Tovey, p.236.
14 Rosen, p.375.
15 Thayer, p.871, quoting the *Harmonicon* for January 1824.

Bibliography

Beethoven, *Missa Solemnis*, Eulenburg Miniature Score, London c.1964, edited with a foreword by Willy Hess; textual notes in German only.

Beethoven, The Letters of, collected, translated and edited by Emily Anderson, 3 vols, London, Toronto and New York, 1961.
Cooper, Martin, *Beethoven, The Last Decade 1817–1827*, London, 1970.
Deane, Basil, *Cherubini*, London and New York, 1965.
Haydn, The Collected Correspondence of Joseph, edited by H.C. Robbins Landon, London and Toronto, 1959.
Kennedy, Michael, *The Hallé Tradition*, Manchester, 1960.
Landon, H.C. Robbins, *Haydn: Chronicle & Works (1796–1800)*, Indiana, 1976; London, 1977.
——*Haydn: Chronicle & Works (1801–1809)*, Indiana, 1976; London, 1977.
New Oxford History of Music, Vol. VII, 'The Age of Enlightenment', London, New York and Toronto, 1973; Edward Olleson's chapter on Church Music deals with the Masses of Mozart and Haydn.
Nottebohm, Gustav, *Zweite Beethoviana*, Leipzig, 1887; New York, 1888; chapter XIX is about the Missa Solemnis sketches.
Riezler, Walter, *Beethoven*, translated by G.D.H. Pidcock, London, 1938; New York, 1972 (paperback).
Rosen, Charles, *The Classical Style: Haydn, Mozart, Beethoven*, London, 1971; New York, 1972.
Schindler, Anton, *Beethoven as I knew him*, translated by Constance S. Jolly from 3rd edition (1860) with notes by Donald MacArdle, London and Chapel Hill, N.C., 1966.
Scholes, Percy, *The Mirror of Music*, 2 vols, London and New York, 1947.
Shaw, H. Watkins, *The Three Choirs Festivals*, Worcester, 1954.
Terry, Sir Richard R., *The Music of the Roman Rite*, London, 1931.

Thayer, Alexander, *A Life of Beethoven*, 3 vols 1866–1879 but incomplete; finished inadequately by various hands in German or English, and admirably in 2 vols revised and edited by Elliott Forbes, Princeton, 1964.

Tovey, Donald Francis, *Essays in Musical Analysis*, Vol.V: 'Vocal Music', London and New York, 1937.

Anon., *A Century and a Half in Soho*, A Short History of the Firm of Novello, 1811–1961, London, 1961.

Bärenreiter publish good miniature scores of the late Haydn Masses and Eulenburg of Beethoven's Mass in C edited by Willy Hess.

Discography

In the days of 78s the Missa Solemnis was virtually ignored by the English record companies. Around 1950 the only complete Masses in the HMV, Columbia and Decca Catalogues were Bach's B minor and two Masses by William Byrd. The advent of LPs changed the situation both quickly and completely. In 1953-4 as many as six Haydn Masses were available on disc, three of them late works (Nos 7, 9 and 12). Beethoven's Mass in C also appeared in 1953 on Vox PL 6300 conducted by Rudolf Moralt. The first two recordings of the Missa Solemnis were both notable:

	UK	USA
Otto Klemperer conducting the Akademie Choir and the Vienna Symphony Orch., with Steingruber, Schuerhoff, Majkut and Wiener	Vox PL6992 (1953)	
Toscanini conducting the Shaw Chorale and the NBC Orch., with Marshall, Merriman, Conley and Hines	HMV ALP1182-3 (1954)	

By 1978 there were eleven recordings available in Britain, all on four sides except for a reissue on two of Klemperer's 1953 version. As the work plays for about 80 minutes the quality on the latter is poor—inevitably—and in spite of its cheapness it cannot be recommended. Five of today's recordings are outstandingly good:

Otto Klemperer: New Philharmonia Chorus & Orch., with Elisabeth Söderström, Marga Höffgen, Waldemar Kmentt and Martti Talvela	HMV SLS922 (1966)	Angel S3679
Karl Böhm: Vienna State Opera Chorus & Vienna Philharmonic Orch., with Margaret Price, Christa Ludwig, Wiesław Ochman and Martti Talvela	DG 2707 080 (1975)	DG 2707 080

	UK	USA
Carlo Maria Giulini: New Philharmonia Chorus and London Philharmonic Orch., with Heather Harper, Janet Baker, Robert Tear and Hans Sotin	HMV SLS989 (1976)	Angel S3836
Georg Solti: Chicago Symphony Orch. & Chorus, with Lucia Popp, Yvonne Minton, Mallory Walker and Gwynne Howell	Decca D87D2 (1978)	
Herbert von Karajan: Vienna Singverein & Berlin Philharmonic Orch., with Gundula Janowitz, Christa Ludwig, Fritz Wunderlich and Walter Berry	DG 2726 048	DG 2707 030

The last of these is a reissue dating from 1966 and much cheaper than the others.

The following recordings are of the other Masses mentioned most frequently in this book:

Beethoven Mass in C:

	UK	USA
Carlo Maria Giulini: New Philharmonic Chorus & Orch., with Elly Ameling, Janet Baker, Theo Altmeyer and Marius Rintzler	HMV ASD2661 (1971)	Angel S36775
Douglas Guest: St John's College Choir (Cambridge) and the Academy of St Martin-in-the-Fields, with Felicity Palmer, Helen Watts, Robert Tear and Christopher Keyte	Decca/Argo ZRG739 (1974)	Decca/Argo ZRG739

Haydn *Missa in tempore belli* (No.7):

	UK	USA
Douglas Guest: St John's College Choir and the Academy of St Martin-in-the-Fields, with April Cantelo, Helen Watts, Robert Tear and Barry McDaniel	Decca/Argo ZRG634 (1970)	Decca/Argo ZRG634

	UK	*USA*
Rafael Kubelik: Bavarian Radio Chorus & Orch., with Elsie Morison, Marjorie Thomas, Peter Witsch and Karl Christian Kohn	DG/Heliodor 2548 229	

This last is a reissue dating from 1964 but of excellent quality and much cheaper than its rival.

Haydn *Nelson* Mass (No.9):

	UK	*USA*
David Willcocks: King's College Choir (Cambridge) and the London Symphony Orch., with Sylvia Stahlmann, Helen Watts, Wilfred Brown and Tom Krause	Decca/Argo ZRG5325 (1962)	Decca/Argo ZRG5325

There are also good recordings of the other late Haydn Masses currently available. All six are on Decca/Argo SDDG341-6 conducted by Guest or in one case (No.9) Willcocks, at a cheaper rate per record.

Index

Ailred, 1
Albrechtsberger, J., 6, 113
Allen, Sir Hugh, 109
Alsager, Thomas, 103–5
Arnold, Samuel, 7n
Artaria (publishers), 6, 20

Bach, C.P.E., 11
Bach, J.S.
  Art of Fugue, 7, 47
  '48' Preludes and Fugues, 47–8
  Mass in B minor, 7, 9, 31, 33, 54n., 108–9
  St Matthew Passion, 28, 105
Bach Choir, 109
Barnby, Joseph, 107
Bartók, Béla, 109
Bassoon, 2, 39, 44, 60, 73, 81, 95–7
  Double Bassoon, 96, 100, 105
Beethoven, Johann van, 22
Beethoven, Karl van, 16, 30, 83
Beethoven, Ludwig van
  Cello Sonatas: Op.69 in A, 8
    Op.102, 17, 50
  Consecration of the House Overture, Op.124, 19, 25, 99
  Creatures of Prometheus, Op.43, 47
  Diabelli Variations, Op.120, 19, 50
  Fidelio, Op.72, 24–5, 88, 99
  Mass in C, Op.86, 4–9, 13, 32–4, 38, 41, 62, 65, 86, 94, 102–3, 106, 108–9
  Mass (in C sharp minor?), 21–2, 96
  Missa Solemnis:
    Autograph, 35–6, 48, 74
    Falling thirds, 34, 40–1, 54, 56, 63, 67, 82, 84, 89
    First performance, 19, 20, 22–6
    Fugal writing, 11, 38–9, 45–50, 55, 65–70, 74–6, 84–5, 89–90
    High notes, 25, 42, 50, 56, 68
    Key contrasts, 36–7, 44–5, 54–5, 72, 79, 81, 88
    Metronome markings (lack of), 101
    Modal touches, 45, 50, 58, 62
    Publication, 20–1, 27, 35, 101, 106–7
    Sketches, 19, 36, 54, 63, 83, 89, 106, 109
    Symbolism, 38, 53, 57, 59–61, 63, 70–1, 74, 77, 85, 92
    Ties over barlines, 34, 39, 45, 48–50, 69, 84, 90, 110
  Piano Concertos: Op.58 in G, 15
    Op.73 in E flat, 15, 88
  Piano Sonatas: Op.81 in E flat, 15
    Op. 106 in B flat, *Hammerklavier*, 15–19, 34, 50–1, 72
    Op.109 in E, 19
    Op.110 in A flat, 19, 47–8, 50
    Op.111 in C minor, 19
  Piano Trios: Op.70, 8
    Op.97 in B flat, 15
  String Quartets: Op.59/3 in C, 50
    Op.131 in C sharp minor, 22, 78, 84
    Op.133, *Grosse Fuge*, 51, 108
    Op.135 in F, 84, 91–2
  Symphonies: No.1, Op.21 in C, 99
    No.3, Op.55 in E flat, *Eroica*, 46
    No.5, Op.67 in C minor, 7, 8, 99
    No.6, Op.68 in F, *Pastoral*, 7, 8, 99
    No.9, Op.125 in D minor, 18–19, 22–3, 27, 34, 65, 92, 94, 96–9
  Triple Concerto, Op.56 in C, 15
  Variations and Fugue, Op.35, 47, 50
  Violin Sonata, Op.96 in G, 15
  Wellington's Victory (*Battle Symphony*), Op.91, 21
Berlioz, Hector, 109
  Symphonie fantastique, 51
  Te Deum, 28
Birmingham, 107
Bonn, 75, 106

Brahms's Third Symphony, 110-1
Breitkopf & Härtel (publishers), 8, 29
Britten's Missa Brevis, 14, 86
Busoni, F., 80

Cellos, 59, 74, 76, 95
Chamberlain, Neville, 91
Cherubini, Luigi, 7, 9, 14
  First Mass, 6
  Mass No.2 in D minor, 6, 109
  Requiem in D minor, 104
Clarinet, 39, 76, 78, 82, 97
Clarke, Charles Cowden, 103, 105
Clement, Franz, 23
Cooper, Martin, 51, 91-2
Costa, Sir Michael, 78, 107
Council of Trent, 2, 62
Czerny, Carl, 47, 106

Deutsch, O.E., 115
Diabelli, Antonio, 19-21

Eisenstadt, 3, 5-7, 86
Elgar's Second Symphony, 83
Esterhazy, Prince Anton, 3
  Prince Nicholas I, 3
  Prince Nicholas II, 3-5, 7

Fitzpatrick, Horace, 97
Fitzwilliam Museum, The, 104
Flute, 59, 74, 76-7, 96-7
Franz (Francis) II, Emperor, 15, 21-2
Fuchs, Johann, 113

Galitzin, Prince Nicholas, 21, 27
George IV, King, 21
Giulini, Carlo Maria, 109
Gounod's Messe Solennelle, 108
Gyrowetz, Adalbert, 113

Haizinger (Haitzinger), Anton, 24
Hallé, Sir Charles, 107-8
Handel, G.F., 7
  Alexander's Feast, 6
  Messiah, 6, 28, 36, 90, 107-9
Haslinger, Tobias, 48
Haydn, Joseph
  Creation, The, 4, 5, 7, 9, 95, 100
  Masses, 8, 9, 13, 65, 72-3, 107
    No.3, Missa St Caecilia, 9
    No.7, Missa in tempore belli, 5, 10,
      12-14, 86-7, 113

No.8, Missa St Bernardi von Offida,
  5, 7, 11, 12, 113
No.9, Missa in angustiis (Nelson), 5,
  7, 10, 11, 13, 32, 56, 80, 95, 103,
  109
No.10, Theresienmesse, 5, 12, 113
No.11, Schöpfungmesse, 5, 13, 59
No.12, Harmoniemesse, 4-6, 10-13
Seasons, The, 7
Haydn, Michael, 2
Hess, Willy, 59, 63, 75
Holmes, Edward, 105-7
Hopkins, E.J., 105
Horns, 5, 38-9, 73, 92, 97-9
Hummel, Johann Nepomuk, 4, 5, 7-9
  Mass in B flat, 9-11, 13, 107-8
  Mass in E flat, 10, 11, 13, 107-8
  Mass in D minor, 107, 113

Joseph II, Emperor, 3

Keats, John, 103
Keeffe, Bernard, 110n
Kinsky, Prince, 16
Klemperer, Otto, 75, 109
Kreutzer, Rudolph, 105
Krug, Walter, 92

Landon, H.C. Robbins, 113-5
Leopold II, Emperor, 15
Lichnowsky, Count Moritz, 21-4
Lobkowitz, Prince Franz Joseph von, 16,
  58
Loraine, R.G., 103
Louis XVIII, King, 21

MacArdle, Donald, 115
Mahler, Gustav, 51, 92, 94
Manchester, 107
Manchester Guardian, The, 107
Mann, Thomas, 114
Massenet, Jules, 31
Mendelssohn, 94, 105, 109
  Elijah, 107-9
Mori, Nicolas, 105
Moscheles, Ignaz, 104-5, 109
Moto Proprio, 2
Mozart, Wolfgang Amadeus
  Masses, 2, 64, 100, 107
    Mass in F, K.192, 65
    Coronation Mass in C, K.317, 6, 10,
      11
    Credo Mass in C, K.257, 65

Organ Solo Mass in C, K.259, 2, 64
Mass in C minor, K.427, 9, 51–2, 115
Requiem, K.626, 7, 78, 115
'Twelfth Mass' (spurious), 108
Musical Times, The, 106–8, 115

Nageli, H.G., 7
Nanini, 6
Napoleonic Wars, 3, 13, 29, 83, 86–8
Nottebohm, Gustav, 106
Novello, Alfred, 104, 107
  Clara, 104–5
  Mary, 105
  Vincent, 65, 105–7
Novello's Vocal Scores, 103, 107

Oboe, 33–4, 44, 67, 84, 96–8
Olleson, Edward, 113
Organ, 59, 100

Palestrina, 1, 2, 6, 9, 62
  Missa Papae Marcellae, 33
  Stabat Mater, 62
Palffy, Count Ferdinand, 23
Pegge, Morley, 97
Peters (publishers), 20
Philharmonic Society of London, The, 18
Pope Benedict XIV, 2
  Pius VII, 17
  Pius X, 2
Preisinger, 24

Radziwill, Prince Anton, 21, 27
Reed, John, 115
Ries, Ferdinand, 20
Riezler, Walter, 31, 33, 35, 46, 85, 91–2
Robertson, Alec, 28, 31
Rode, Pierre, 16
Rosen, Charles, 31, 71, 112
Rossini, Giacomo, 100
Rudolph, Archduke, 7, 15–17, 19–21, 26, 30–1, 76
Russia, Czar of, 21

St Petersburg, 20, 27
Salzburg, Archbishop Hieronymus Colloredo of, 2
Schiller, Friedrich von, 29
Schindler, Anton, 6, 16–17, 20–2, 24–6, 35, 65–6, 75, 93, 101, 106
Schlemmer (publishers), 24
Schlesinger (publishers), 19, 20
Schmidt-Görg, Dr Joseph, 36

Schoenberg, Arnold, 51
Scholes, Percy, 108–9
Schott (publishers), 27, 101
Schubert, Franz, 31, 107, 109, 113
  Auf dem Strom, 97
  Mass in A flat, 110
  Mass in E flat, 108, 110
  Symphony No.9 in C, 100
Schulz, Edward, 48, 112
Schumann, Robert, 111
  Clara, 111
Schuppanzigh, Ignaz, 22–4
Second Vatican Council, 1, 31
Seipelt, Josef, 24
Shaw, Bernard, 108
Shaw, Watkins, 108
Simrock (publishers), 20
Smyth, Ethel, 14, 86, 112
Sontag, Henriette, 22, 26
Spohr, Louis, 104, 106
  The Last Judgment, 109
Stravinsky's Mass, 11n., 14

Tayber, Anton, 21
Tchaikovsky, 109
Terry, Sir Richard R., 113
Thayer, A.W., 6, 19, 28
Three Choirs Festivals, 102–3, 108–9
Times, The, 104
Timpani, 35, 38, 74, 79, 81, 87–9, 92, 99
Tolbecque, A.J., 105
Tovey, Donald Francis, 28, 32–3, 35, 59, 62, 70, 77–8, 91–2, 112
Trombones, 40, 44, 48, 55, 63–4, 71, 73, 78, 96, 99, 100
Trumpets, 5, 38, 73, 81, 87–9, 92, 99
Tuscher, Baron von, 6

Umlauf, Ignaz, 24–5
Unger, Karoline, 22, 25–6

Vaughan Williams, Ralph, 111
Victoria, 6
Violas, 58–9, 74, 76, 95
Violins, 55, 63, 74, 83, 92, 94–6
  Solo violin, 77–80

Wagner, Richard, 51
Weber, Carl Maria von, 14, 100, 107
Weber, Franz, 106
Whitman, Walt, 111

York, 106

Zelter, C.F., 105

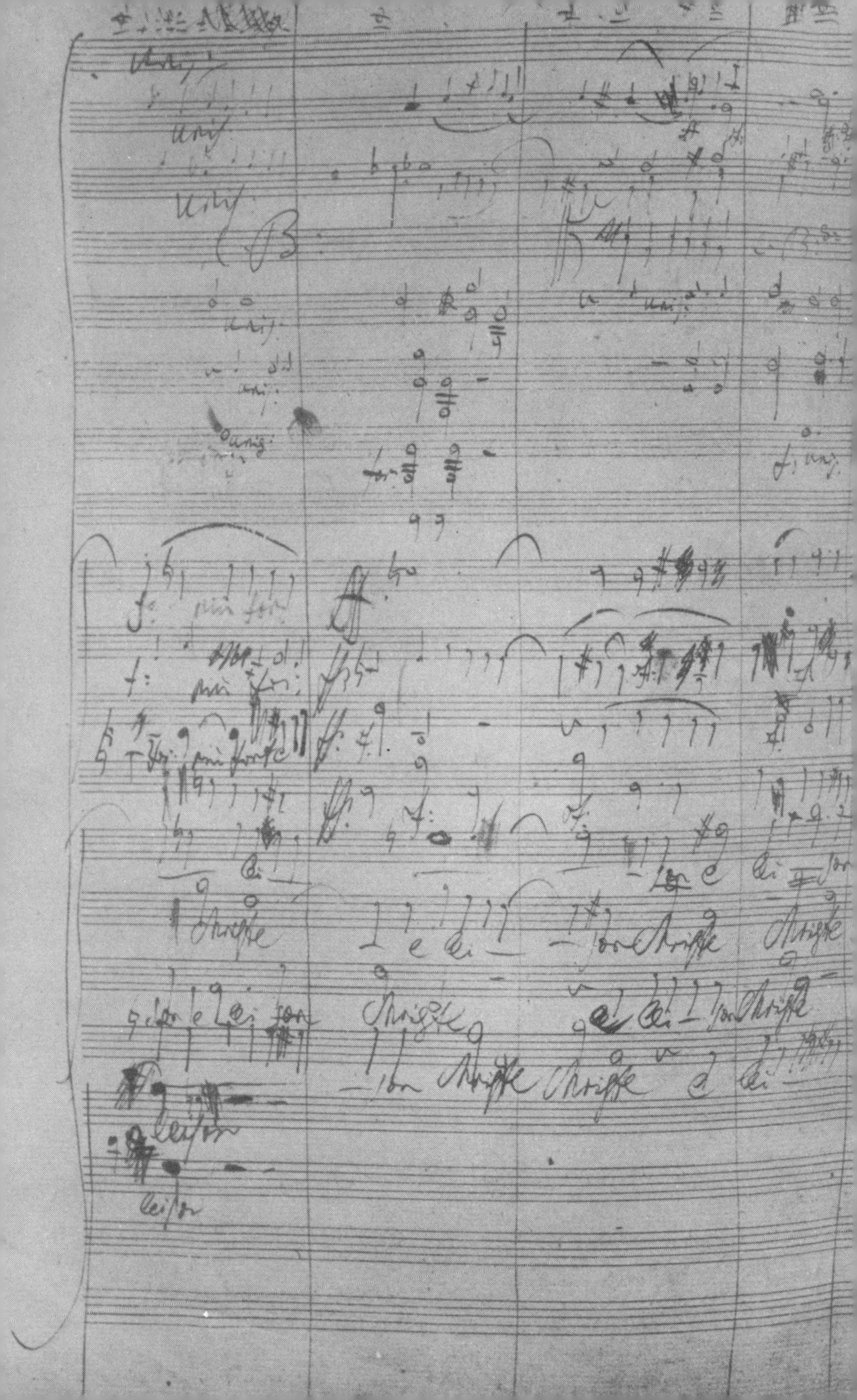

unis.
piu forte
Christe
eleison
leison